RICHARD G. LUG
UNITED STATES SENATOR
WASHINGTON, D.C. 20510

March 26, 2012

Dr. Peggy Hinckley
Superintendent
Warren Township Schools
975 North Post Road
Indianapolis, Indiana 46219

Dear Peggy:

I wanted to take a moment to share my deep admiration and appreciation for your service as Superintendent of Warren Township Schools after learning that you intend to retire at the end of this school year.

Talented school leaders are crucial to creating an academic environment that helps drive success, and the dramatic improvements at Warren Township during your tenure are truly remarkable. During my visits with teachers and education leaders both in Indiana and in Washington, D.C., I have been pleased to share your reforms as an example of how to close the achievement gap.

I likewise appreciate your leadership in promoting energy efficiency within your school corporation. Improving our nation's energy security has long been one of my foremost policy priorities, and I have enthusiastically touted your success when speaking about the issue of energy conservation. I am confident that the conservation habits your students have developed will be shared and have an impact well beyond the classroom.

Thank you, again, for your service. I wish you every continuing success in your future endeavors and look forward to meeting again.

Sincerely,

Richard G. Lugar
United States Senator

RGL/cbc

Not Paid For at Government Expense.
Printed on Recycled Paper.

MONITORING

KEEPING YOUR FINGER ON THE PULSE OF SCHOOL IMPROVEMENT

Peggy Hinckley, Ed.D.

Published & distributed by:
Peggy Hinckley, Ed.D.

in association with:
IBJ Book Publishing
41 E. Washington St., Suite 200
Indianapolis, IN 46204
www.ibjbp.com

www.peggyhinckley.com

ISBN 978-1-934922-80-4
First Edition

Library of Congress Control Number: 2012941179

Printed in the United States of America

DEDICATION

To the educators of the MSD of Warren Township, Indianapolis, Indiana, who embraced the Eight Step Continuous Improvement Process, improving the academic achievement for all children and now lead other Indiana educators in this change initiative;

To the MSD of Warren Township Board of Education, who had the courage to demand more from us and hold us accountable;

To Pat Davenport, for teaching us all how to be more effective educators and leaders;

To Katy, Mark, Denise, and Tom, for their loving support and tireless belief in my ability to do the work.

TABLE OF CONTENTS

FOREWORD

If you are a superintendent, central office administrator, building principal or classroom teacher this is a book that will change the way you think about managing instruction-at the district, school and classroom level.

In my twelve years of teaching the Plan-Do-Check-Act /Eight Step Process to educators across the nation the piece that is often not implemented correctly is the "Check" or Step 8-monitoring.

School teams attend the week- long training on the Eight Step Process, effectively put the continuous improvement model in place but fail to act or check at frequent intervals and are then disappointed that the results do not validate the hard work principals and teachers have invested to raise student performance.

Daily consistent monitoring of whether or not instruction is working is critical to the success of any school or district.

Peggy Hinckley takes the reader through the importance of monitoring in this easy to read, practical book. Dr. Hinckley has lived it in her 32 years of administrative experience and she takes the reader from theory to practice. It makes a great book study for all educators and a road map to insure that hard effort on the part of the superintendent, district administrative staff, principals, teachers and students is reflected in the data.

Patricia Davenport
Educational Consultant
Patricia Davenport Consulting, LLC

CHAPTER ONE

YOU
WANT ME
TO DO
WHAT?

HAVE you ever heard the saying, "People respect what we inspect?" How many times have you, as an educator, participated in training, went back to your classroom or school and tried to implement, ran into problems, and just stopped. The shocking truth—no one ever checked! They just assumed you were implementing with success. Wasted money, time, and no real school improvement.

As school districts struggle with state and federal accountability measures, leadership in those districts identify solutions to their achievement gaps, hopeful that these solutions will produce better student achievement results. The solutions and the rationale behind their selection may not have trickled down to the classroom teacher level, producing the cry, **"You want me to do what?"** And all at once, the mountains of research about why individuals resist change becomes the night stand reading for all administrators.

The failure to address achievement gaps with a viable solution has tremendous ramifications. There is no audience for blaming parents or societal forces that negatively impact our students. But just citing those state or federal ramifications is not enough. We must engage educators to understand the moral implications of failing to close achievement gaps with a solution that makes sense to those educators. Our typical response is to let educators know the training dates, hold the training, and wish everyone well in implementing. Even if there is an implementation plan, how effectively is it communicated? Most importantly, we fail to monitor the plan, making adjustments based on educator feedback, problem solving based on unique building or district issues, conflict resolution when educators struggle with the change initiative, and providing feedback to the buildings on their proper implementation of the elements of the solution.

Our problem in education is not the lack of solutions. It is the random act of school improvement initiatives with **no monitoring.** Further, we keep adopting solutions year after year, failing to prune those solutions that have not proven their worth. With no monitoring of the solutions, we have no data to determine what has rooted and proven itself in results versus one more program that complicates the teacher day with no results to prove it works. Principals and teachers are weary of this cycle of dysfunction.

The purpose of this book is to change that cycle. First of all, assess the effectiveness of your current school improvement efforts by looking at data for results. Conduct that audit with your principals and teacher leadership. Listen, as painful as it may be, to hear their feedback. Keep those initiatives that are working and have the courage to end those that are ineffective. As you look to fill the holes with a meaningful solution, create an implementation plan and then, most importantly, **create a monitoring plan of how you will trust but verify that the elements of the solution are being implemented properly. Accept that the monitoring will be a commitment for as long as you use the program, not a one year plan.**

W. Edwards Deming believed variation was wasteful. The total quality management movement framed the notion that when you reduce variation in the system, you produce a more consistent result. Monitoring reduces that variation in your change effort so results are consistent.

My own experience in implementing solutions over 28 years as a superintendent taught me that implementation of a solution is not just hard work. It is also a political process that, if not managed well, can destroy your solution. If you do not address the problems that always arise in implementing anything, the problems will destroy the solution.

Educators want to do the right thing, but when their implementation issues cannot be addressed, they fall away from the elements of the solution until it is eventually abandoned. The results we are counting on never materialize. I learned that even after ten years of implementing an eight step continuous improvement process (Davenport, 2006), we found gaps in implementation of the steps that affected results. This was particularly evident when we had weak building level leadership that allowed the adults in the school to fashion the solution to meet adult needs, not those of the students. Without monitoring each and every year for over a decade, we would not have sustained impressive results in student achievement that our educators led that kept us focused on the critical elements of the implementation plan.

Doug Reeves (2011) identified in *Finding* Your *Leadership Focus* three essential practices - focus, monitoring, and efficacy – that positively influence student achievement.

We have found three essential clusters of leadership practices that positively impact student achievement: focus, monitoring, and efficacy. By "focus" we mean that leaders identify and monitor no more than six priority instructional initiatives that are linked clearly to specific student needs. By "monitoring" we mean the regular (typically at least once per quarter) systematic observation of adult actions—what teachers and leaders do in order to improve student learning. By "efficacy" we mean the personal conviction of teachers and administrators that their actions are the primary influences on the academic success of students. (pg. 26)

Given his research, it is clear that the success of any school improvement initiative is **monitoring.**

This book outlines specific monitoring skill sets for all educators engaged in school improvement solutions. These skills are not specific to any one initiative but apply to any change effort a school or district may be implementing. The chapter outlines are as follows:

■ Chapter 2—Confronting Adult Comfort Zones vs. Needs of Students

No Child Left Behind (NCLB) has made educational systems move past the traditional averages and confront the brutal truth of subgroup achievement levels. That forced emphasis uncovered a little secret: children of race and ethnicity, poverty, and gender were not achieving at comparable levels to the averages. And as the change solution addresses the data, it also gets into adult comfort levels. Doing what is in the best interest of the children is now causing conflict with the culture of the way things have always been done.

■ Chapter 3 – The "Oprah" Moment: It is Always About Relationships and Influence

When we want others to change their professional practice, we must connect through our relationships with them. Making that connection assumes a past relationship in some way. If there is none, then the leader must take an extraordinary amount of time to visit those classrooms, connect to those educators by listening to their concerns, making the case of why this plan will address those concerns, being willing to make adjustments in the plan if the feedback overwhelmingly dictates a change, and gaining support for the change. Leaders must be a credible source of knowledge on the change effort in their own right because teachers will test that knowledge and expect leaders to pass the test. A leader without this critical knowledge base will influence no one.

■ Chapter 4 – Teacher Leadership: The Secret Ingredient

Any change effort must make its case to teachers and teacher leaders, convincing them that the change will pass their test of common sense, making it better for the students they serve. Once teachers are convinced the change will make a difference in improving student achievement and they see the results, teachers will embrace the change, make it a part of their routine, and make adjustments that will further improve the implementation of the change effort. Without teacher support, no change effort will ever root. Teacher leaders must be embraced by the administration, be a part of the refinements in the change process, and lead the charge among their peers for better daily practices.

■ Chapter 5 – Monitoring: Troubleshooting, Problem Solving, and Paying Close Attention

Leaders sometimes believe just because they say it, educators will follow. Leaders must monitor the change by establishing the nonnegotiables of the effort, observing and discussing those nonnegotiables to determine compliance, checking for transfer of the learning of the training to the classroom, and checking for the consistency of classroom implementation within the school. This is the step frequently ignored that becomes the root cause to the downfall of the change effort. Monitoring is not only the responsibility of the building leaders, including teachers, but also the district leaders. They must confront problems with solutions, involving educators. They must confront those who are not compliant with the established nonnegotiable elements of the change and have the difficult conversations. Without this step, the leader is doomed to fail.

■ Chapter 6 – When Trouble Persists: Having the Difficult Conversations

The easiest role of a leader is being able to say "yes" or affirm the teacher behaviors that support increased student achievement. The most difficult role of a leader is confronting classroom practices and educator attitudes that are outside the elements of the implementation plan for the change effort. Confrontation is unpleasant and assumes a knowledge base that can address the lack of implementation or attitude. But without these conversations, the blockers of the change effort gain momentum because they get away with being noncompliant.

■ Chapter 7 – Student Monitoring of Their Learning

Teachers complain about the lack of personal responsibility by students for their learning. When teacher decisions are driven by data, students are taught to own their data and assume responsibility for doing whatever the teacher prescribes to correct their learning deficits.

■ Chapter 8 – Celebrations: By the Inch is a Cinch, By the Yard is Too Hard

Recognition is affirmation of effort in producing positive change and is a motivator to continue the effort. Leaders must celebrate every inch of progress whether it is individual praise or praise focused on the group. When we define the smaller steps within the parameters of the change, we must not only pay attention to those that are not implementing, but celebrate those who are making strides toward the change effort.

■ Chapter 9 – Maintaining Momentum and Building Ownership within the Culture

Once schools and districts gain momentum through successful steps on their way to the change outcome, they must not assume the change effort is rooted. Otherwise, adults will drift back to what is in the best interests of the adults and not in the best interest of children. Their key is building ownership among educators for the change effort. Once they own the data as not good or bad data, but the next teaching decision, they assume ownership and continue to make refinements to improve the change effort, not abandon it. The change effort is now institutionalized as the way educators do their work.

■ Chapter 10 – District Leadership vs. Building Leadership: Teamwork!

District leaders, in creating a vision for the change effort, must make certain not only that their principals understand and buy into the change plan, but also have the necessary training to gain confidence in implementing and monitoring the nonnegotiables. District leaders cannot issue the order of a new change effort and then get out of the way with principals. They must work alongside of them, in classrooms, to understand the implementation struggles and have opportunities to dialogue about implementation issues.

These chapters revolve around experiences from educators in the field. While I am not a researcher, many of these practices have been written about by other researchers. I would like to think of my experiences and those of my colleagues as action research – what works from those of us who have lived the life of implementing solutions and sustaining change over time.

I have also included references to the 2011 Educational Leadership Constituents Council (ELCC) Building and District Level Standards as prescribed by the National Policy Board for Educational Administration (2002). If this book is used in a university class, the standards noted at the beginning of each chapter can help to guide the learning.

Each chapter ends with possible scenarios for use in discussions in your school corporation or university classroom. Learning to think on your feet is a key administrative skill. We make hundreds of decisions every day, with many of those on the spot. Further, sometimes what appears to be an issue is not the root cause issue. Rich discussion on the scenarios will build understanding and develop competency in influencing others in the change process.

As you reflect on monitoring your school improvement plan, realize that implementing any change effort requires **courage.** Courage to introduce the change effort, courage to teach others the elements of the change effort, courage to face the doubters, courage to carry on during the stormy recalibration of the school environment, and courage to make the tough decisions. All of the educators in Warren Township had courage to try something different, stay the course through difficult times, and embrace a new way of educating their students through the Eight Step Continuous Improvement Process.

I leave you with the most powerful advice I received from Pat Davenport, who was our teacher in Warren Township with the Eight Steps and has taught the process to thousands of educators across the country. She told me in "year one" that **the first year only happens one time.** Once educators get to the second year, it resembles the behaviors they used in the first year. Everything gets easier.

Never forget as you survive your first year of implementation: fearlessly monitor, cheerlead others, and never compromise what is in the best interests of the children we serve.

CHAPTER TWO

CONFRONTING ADULT COMFORT ZONES VS. NEEDS OF STUDENTS

ELCC Building and District Level Standards: 1.1, 1.2, 2.1, 2.2, 2.3, 3.5, 4.1, 5.1

NO Child Left Behind (NCLB) has required educational systems to move beyond reporting averages and confronting the brutal truth of subgroup achievement levels. Moving beyond averages has uncovered a little secret that we have been underserving children of color and poverty. While many districts remained in denial, telling staff to "ignore that man behind the curtain," they have struggled to find a solution for improving student achievement for those subgroup students. In some cases, schools and districts have remained gridlocked in remembering a time in the past when children came to school ready to learn with stable two parent families. The societal changes, particularly poverty, have changed those districts, but educators continue to use strategies that no longer fit the needs of their students. We must be able to teach the children we have, not the one we used to have or the ones we wish we had.

NCLB has directed state departments of education to disaggregate data by subgroups, moving beyond the averages. In some states, like Indiana, achievement on state assessments is only the beginning of the measurement of school effectiveness. Now the growth model is an additional indicator of performance, determining whether low, medium, or high growth has occurred with a student population, including special attention to the lowest 25%. These new calculations of accountability have challenged educators to develop interventions to address these achievement gaps.

When I was hired in the MSD of Warren Township, Indianapolis, Indiana, in 2001, I was specifically recruited to improve student achievement. In the 1980's, Warren had been the middle class, mostly white, hard-working factory workers that sent their children to school prepared to learn. When I arrived in 2001, we were still teaching those children. But the desegregation order in the 1980's had integrated our community with the additional impact of the economic downturn of the east side of Indianapolis with factory closings, taking with them the lucrative job market. We kept using the same strategies of 20 years ago, in spite of the fact that the children sitting in our classrooms lacked the necessary prerequisite skills to learn our content and some found survival a daily struggle.

I remember a fine math teacher who had taught through the changes. In observing his classroom, I realized there was an invisible line down the middle of the room. He was turned to the left of the room, ever so slightly, focusing on the mostly white, remaining school smart students. On the right side of the imaginary line were the special education students and students of color. They were not receiving the necessary attention to their educational needs. He was a good person and had been a good teacher. He had not made the transition to using formative achievement data to attend to the learning needs of his students. His classroom data and the school data reflected this dated perspective of serving all students.

Larry Lezotte, of Effective Schools fame, once taught me that if a district were to engage in continuous improvement, they must have a continuous data stream. As he and Kathleen McKee point out in *Assembly Required: A Continuous School Improvement System (2002)*, "schools must develop data-driven systems for monitoring student learning that are much more specific and frequent if they are going to succeed on the mission of 'learning for all.'" (p.6)

So as a principal, central office administrator, teacher leader, or superintendent, how do I begin that conversation using the data without making it a personal attack? How do I use data to create a

Spring 2011 RPMS AYP Performance Categories

English Performance

	2010		2011	
	pass%	target %	pass%	target %
Overall	72.5	68.7	72.2	75.4
Black	66.2	66.2	62.1	72.1
Hispanic	NA	NA	62.1	67.1 safe harbor
White	76.2	67.1	78.5	73.8
F/R Meals	69.2	67.3	65.2	74.3
LEP	NA	NA	60	67.4 safe harbor
SP ED	49.3	63.8	43.9	69.1

Math Performance

	2010		2011	
	pass%	target %	pass%	target %
Overall	76.3	67.5	76.4	74.5
Black	67.7	65	62.1	71.2
Hispanic	NA	NA	74.1	66.2
White	81.6	65.9	84.8	72.9
F/R Meals	72.5	66.2	71.1	73.4
LEP	NA	NA	75	66.4
SP ED	51.4	62.5	53.7	68.2 safe harbor

Figure 2.1 A typical data picture for a school (Raymond Park Middle School)

mirror for the educator, showing the impact, or lack of it, of their instruction? How do principals create data walls to track the progress of students as they either improve or decline?

School, Grade and Classroom Data Points

Most districts have access to disaggregated data on standardized assessments for their schools through their respective state departments of education because of the requirements of NCLB. The key is using that standardized data to bring a sense of urgency to the faculty so they see the logic in the solution being offered. Further, formative assessment data must be in place to have a continuous improvement system to drive teaching decisions. The data appeals to their moral purpose to educate children to high levels of achievement. It helps them come to terms with a distorted view of their success by ignoring the subgroups. The data is their reality. It does not lie. It does not offer

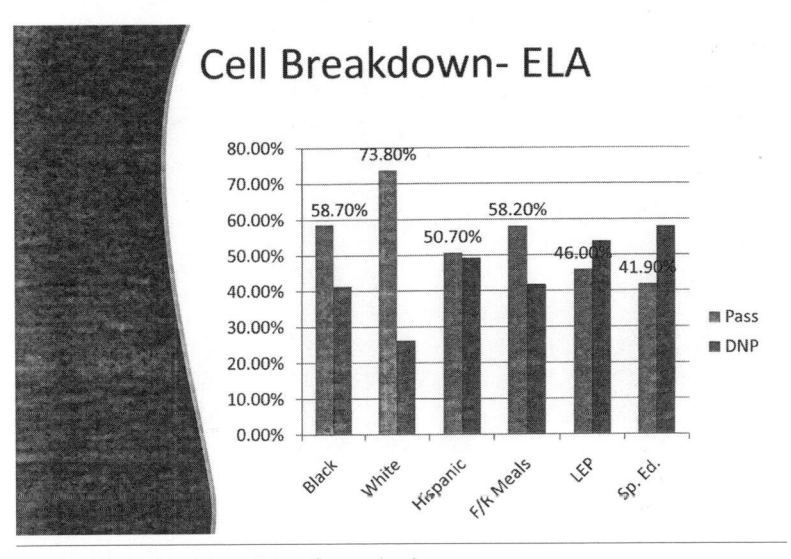

Figure 2.2 A typical data picture for a school

excuses. It tells the truth with no sugar coating. It is not about good data or bad data. It tells us which teaching decision to make next.

As we look at this data picture, our questions to the staff might be as follows:

- *Which children are achieving at acceptable levels in math or language arts?*
- *How far above the standard are they achieving?*
- *Which children are not meeting the standard in math or language arts?*
- *How far below the standard are they achieving?*
- *In which specific skills are children succeeding?*
- *In which skills are they failing to succeed?*
- *Are there any specific curricular areas where our school or grade level is failing to master? How will our solution address those areas with extra emphasis?*
- *What are our attendance rates for this group?*
- *How many discipline referrals and what are the patterns?*
- *How many suspensions are these children experiencing?*

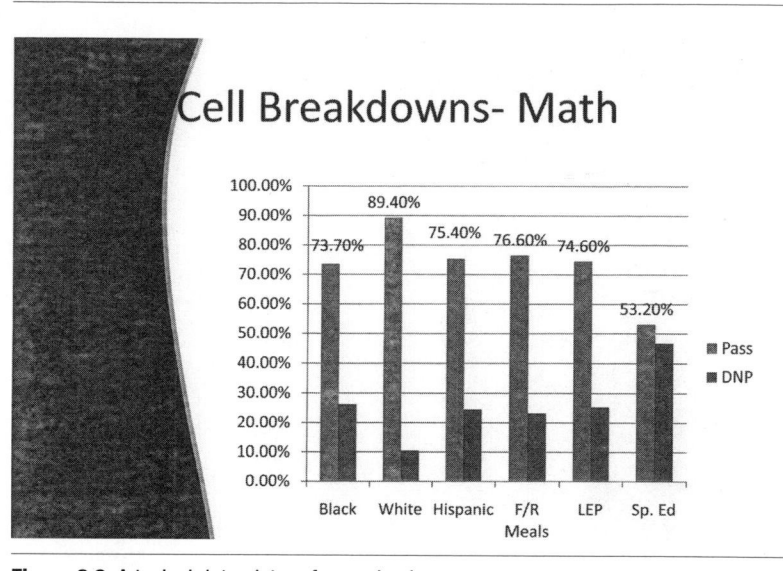

Figure 2.3 A typical data picture for a school

The conversation then moves to classroom data. Teachers look at their own individual data, using their class lists, and determine specific student profiles.

- *Which students have met the standard in math and language arts?*
- *By how much?*
- *Which students have failed to meet the standards? What are their names and how close or far were they from the standard?*
- *What standards had the strongest scores? The weakest?*
- *What adjustments in my teaching do I need to make to meet student needs?*

Teachers then take state assessment data, along with benchmark data like DIBELS and Acuity, and create a data wall. (**Figure 2.4**) The data wall includes a sticky note for each child with test data and other information such as special education services, EL services, etc. The bands are colors ranging from the top band of blue, for above average mastery, green for mastery, yellow for partial mastery, and red for non-mastery. This is a powerful visual for teachers to see student progress, or lack of it. **The data wall is always in a secure place away from the eyes of children or parents, since it contains**

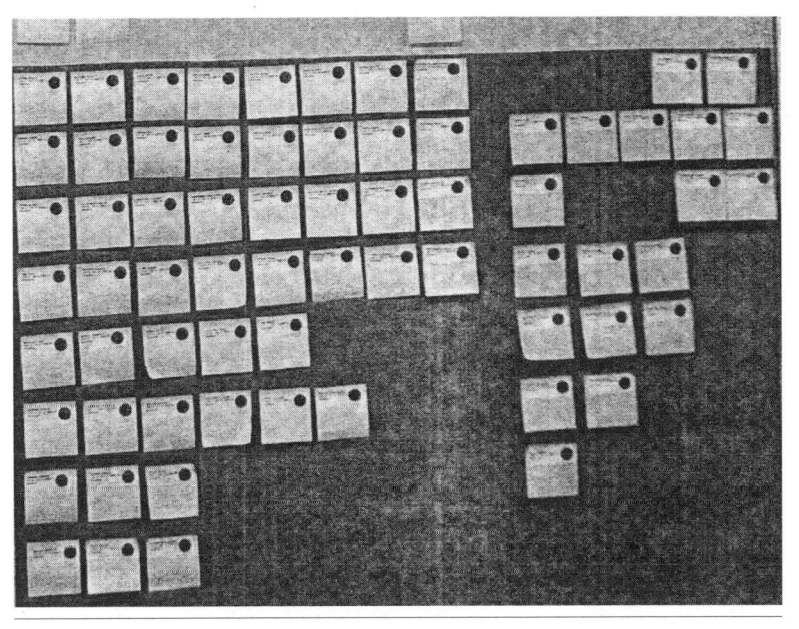

Figure 2.4 Data wall – Hawthorne Elementary School

student names. Names move up with progress or down with loss of progress.

It is not only important to understand who passed and who failed, but by how much. Pat Davenport, who trained our schools in the Eight Step Continuous Improvement Process and worked with us for over a decade, taught us about the instructional group in **Figure 2.5**.

These groups help teachers to structure groups for instruction. That instruction will vary in intensity, based on how far or close the student scores to the acceptable cut score. Please know that focusing on just "bubble kids" may temporarily improve scores. You must focus on building capacity with all children to produce sustainable results.

The critical next step for a principal is having individual classroom teacher conversations about their data. Teachers must work through their own data so they know it. It represents the year prior, in most cases. But the data trends can inform and instruct the work for the following year. They can learn what they need to emphasize more in the standards and may look at the instructional strategies they

Instructional Groups[1]

Instructional groups are defined to categorize results and share a common language, NOT to label students.

Groups	Description
Mastery Students	Students who perform exceptionally in every testing area.
System Students	Students who should perform exceptionally, but just missed the test objective or mastery standard.
Bubble Students	Students who need to work in specific skill areas and are candidates for special tutoring.
Reteach Students	Students who did not grasp the material and need intensive remediation instruction. (Investigate whether the teaching method used could be a contributing factor.)
Foundation Students	Students who are identified and/or eligible for special education.

Figure 2.5 Instructional Groups (Eight Step Training Manual)

used to determine their effectiveness. But nothing makes a greater impression on teachers then the comparison of scores of their class list from this year to last year (**Figure 2.6**).

One of our principals, Ryan Russell, took student data for a class, identified their incoming scores from the year before, and analyzed for each teacher the progress of each student, or lack of it. In several cases, teachers we would have deemed highly effective had a negative impact on the achievement of individual children. When conscientious teachers see this data, they are always stunned, reflective, and immediately vow

Raymond Park Intermediate Academy

Instructional Effectiveness Information Sheet

Teacher:

Before they Entered Your Classroom	Pass	DNP	% Passing
English Language Arts	17	7	70.83%
Math	18	6	75%

After Your Instruction	Pass	DNP	% Passing
English Language Arts	20	4	83.33%
Math	13	11	54.16%

*Only Students Enrolled 162+ Days in your Classroom have been included in this data

INSTRUCTIONAL EFFECTIVENESS	Before	After	Effectiveness
English Language Arts	70.83%	83.33%	12.5%
Math	75%	54.16%	-20.84%

Figure 2.6 Instructional Effectiveness Information Sheet – Ryan Russell, Raymond Park Intermediate Academy

to change that pattern. It forces us to deal with what the data tells us, not what our impressions or biases tell us. Sometimes the most effective teachers are the ones we would never predict to be so.

Using Formative Assessments to Drive Teaching Decisions

In using test data results, a picture of achievement strengths and weaknesses can be drawn. But that picture only tells you the past. It does not help your teaching staff change their instruction to fit the immediate learning needs of students. You need data as teachers move through their curriculum to assess their effectiveness in the moment.

The school improvement solution you have selected must have formative assessments to measure progress as teachers move through the state standards, or new core standards. Formative means "to shape or develop." These assessments can take many forms. Without short, informal assessments to measure the effectiveness of the lesson, teachers are cheated out of the information that can make their instruction more effective.

In the traditional classroom, teachers teach the lesson, assign homework, and eventually give a summative, or final assessment. The grades are recorded in the grade book and the teacher moves on to the next lesson. What's wrong with that? If I did not understand the lesson, I remain confused. There is no process for the teacher to provide further instruction to assist me, known as remediation or tutoring, or even extend the learning through enrichment. Further, what data can a principal use from this model to help a teacher become more effective? Homework grades? End of unit test scores?

As our district has used the Eight Step Process, our teachers use teacher-developed three week formative assessments that measure standards taught in a three week calendar window. The assessments give each classroom teacher in those curricular areas ongoing data to make adjustments in their instruction, provide tutoring or remediation, and work on reviewing those standards that seemed problematic to students. Once again, the ongoing formative assessments give teachers objective data on mastery of standards to base their next teaching decisions. They meet every three weeks as a grade level with their principal to review the data. Every teacher's data is on the screen, color coded based on mastery as green, yellow, or red. After the initial discomfort, teachers learn to talk about effective strategies, what students need further teaching, what enrichment can be provided to those who mastered, and highlight individual students who are improving or deteriorating. (**Figure 2.7**)

One of the painful elements of confronting our brutal truth with data is that it uncovers what adults sometimes do because it is easier or more convenient but not necessarily in the best interests of students. Using data forces educators to confront those ineffective adult behaviors that impede progress.

Why is this formative data important? It gives teachers and principals real time data as the year proceeds about effectiveness. It allows the teacher to evaluate strategies and use the data to make teaching decisions. Think of the power of ongoing data to improve teaching

No.	ELL	IEP	Gen	Eth	Class List	1.5.4	1.6.6	1.2.6	1.1.6					
									MSD OF WARREN TOWNSHIP					
					3 Week Block				Mastery of State Academic Standards – 2011-12 End Date:					
					4A				LEARNING LOG					
								Teacher:			Grade: 1st		Logs due:	
					M: Mastery (85% or higher)				P: Partial-Mastery			N: Non-Mastery (74% or l		
					Working at expected level of IN Academic Standards				Partial Mastery (75%-84%)			Working below expected level		
					Language Arts				**Standards and Indicators**					

No.	ELL	IEP	Gen	Eth	Class List	1.5.4	1.6.6	1.2.6	1.1.6					
1					Elijah	P	M	N						
2					Keona	M	M	N						
3					Kelly	P	M	P						
4					Sofarro	P	N	N						
5					Savannah	M	M	M						
6					Christa	M	M	N						
7					Ethan	P	M	P						
8					Olivia	M	M	N						
9					Kennedy	M	M	N						
10					Makyla	M	M	P						
11					Lee	P	M	P						
12					Shapaira	P	M	N						
13					Makila	P	M	N						
14					Giovanni	P	M	N						
15					Logan	M	M							
16					Kaitlyn	M	M	N						
17					Kahlie	N	P	P						
18					Anthony	M	N	N						
19					Blake	P	M	N						
20					Brayon	M	M	N						
21					Kemu									
22					Brandon	N	P	N						
23					Daylnn	P	M	N						
24					La'Bron	P	N	N						
25					Michelle	P	N	N						
26														
27														
28														
29														
30														
31														
					M	10	18	1						
					P	13	3	5						
					N	2	4	18						

Figure 2.7 Formative data shared during a learning log meeting – Eastridge Elementary

performance. Another lesson I learned long ago from Larry Lezotte was that you could not be a continuous improvement district without a continuous data stream. Formative assessments give you that ability.

This ritual of reflection is similar to the one used by medical professionals. At the shift change, nurses review the current patient data, like our formative assessments, look at their own observational notes, and make a professional judgment about the next course of treatment. Teachers can use formative assessment data in the same manner.

Communication

Even over time, some ideas remain critical to implementing change. When Peters and Waterman wrote *In Search of Excellence* in 1982, they used the frame "ready-fire-aim" as the action plan to describe America's best run companies. They spurred us to action rather than talking about it. We have to do something. They warned us about "fat plans." As we look at communicating the change solution, we must be able to describe a clear picture of the elements of the plan, what you want to see, and why this solution will address the problems identified in Chapter 2 through the data analysis. Don't leave that portion to the training. It must be communicated by the leader. That solution must address what educators believe are the root cause of the problem of achievement, for example. They must believe it has a chance to succeed. Educators must see that if you implement this solution, the experience of the learner will be different.

When discussing the change solution, it is important to demonstrate respect for what has been done in the past. Educators were doing the best of what they knew. But now, as the data drives a different decision, the logic is that the data requires a different solution. Presenting the solution, allowing staff to question the elements of the solution, and providing the training for the new solution moves the staff forward.

That does not mean you won't face resistance to the idea. When I faced that resistance in Warren to the Eight Step process, I asked each building if they had a plan, different from what they were doing, that would improve our student achievement results. Of course, they had no plan. They just did not want to do my plan. That is why you just have to get started.

Every leader learns that the story attributed to Casey Stengel is true. He is said to have reported, "Every day on my team I have five players who love me, five who hate me, and fifteen players on the fence. My job as a manager is to keep the fifteen on the fence with the five who love me." You know the five educators who will immediately embrace the idea. Watch how you treat the five who immediately fold their arms and complain. The remaining fifteen are watching how you deal with those who are fighting you. Respect builds trust and better relationships.

Engage educators in the discussion about the change solution. Be clear about non-negotiables, or elements that are critical to the success of the change solution. Listen to every concern. You must be positive and genuinely sincere about your confidence that the change solution will work. Reassure staff that they can accomplish this solution. And begin.

When we implemented the Eight Step process, our non-negotiables were the use of the instructional calendars, three week assessments, Success Period, and participation in the learning log meetings. I said it every year at opening day for eleven years and principals reinforced it regularly. Year after year.

When you begin, look for small wins and reinforce every behavior you can that looks like the new non-negotiable skills. The gains will be small. Implementing something new is like starting a new diet. It sounds like a good idea until the first day you give up the hamburger for the salad. And the gains seem so far away. Even if they do not believe it, ask them to act like it. When they try, they will be surprised at how quickly they will make progress. The role of the leader is to praise, encourage, solve problems, listen to complaints and find a way for that individual to move forward, Treat it as a learning period. Don't criticize. Keep two-way communication flowing and keep refining the solution and its implementation. The leader must be a learner, too. When we solve problems with educators, everyone takes ownership of the solution and its implementation. And remember, problems are our opportunity to demonstrate our best efforts!

Here are some questions to begin your discussions:

- *Share with me how _____ is going.*
- *What problems are you experiencing?*
- *Would you be comfortable sharing your frustration at our next meeting?*
- *What do you think might solve this problem?*
- *I noticed that you were trying _____. How is that working?*
- *Thanks for making the effort. Once you keep doing it, it will get easier.*
- *How have the students responded to the new _____?*
- *What changes have you seen in student engagement?*
- *What results have you experienced?*

By engaging people in the discussion, you are collaborating on a common vision.

If the change solution is the priority, you cannot stop talking about it. It must be a part of your daily conversation with teachers as you visit their classrooms. It must be on the agenda of your teacher meetings. But the communication must be around the actions you are observing, or not observing, in the implementation of the change solution. And accept that for as long as you implement this change solution, you must continue to communicate the priority, the non-negotiables, and your expectation of performance. When leaders stop talking about a change solution, educators assume it is no longer a priority and begin to drift. Pretty soon the change solution is lost.

You can anticipate, after the initial efforts to implement, the buildup of pressure and anger. This build up can be lessened if the leader is constantly communicating. But sometimes the district effort with a change solution makes individual buildings feel a loss of control. When anger builds, you must vent it or it will explode, destroying the effort.

During the first year of our implementation of the Eight Steps, teachers were struggling with calendars, three week assessments, the daily Success Period, and three week learning log meetings. We were asking them to implement a huge change. Teachers contacted their union and really ramped up the pressure to stop. My solution was to go to each building with the union president (divide and conquer, dismantle the mob mentality), listen to their complaints, and answer their questions. I always had the individual building data with me, which in most cases was not very good. Some of the venting became personal with an unsettled teacher contract. When questions turned into "we don't want to do this," I showed them their school data, asked them what they proposed to do instead of the Eight Steps (and they could not go back to what got us in trouble to begin with), and heard silence. They didn't know what else to do. They just didn't want to do the Eight Steps. I let them vent, picked them up, brushed off their knees, and reassured them that I knew they could implement this on behalf of the children who so desperately needed this improvement. And we just kept going.

However, I learned to listen carefully during that venting process to true concerns from teachers and principals. They were concerned about the quality of the formative assessments. While today our teachers develop those as grade levels, our first attempt was made by two well-intentioned teachers who did them in isolation. I incorrectly thought I was saving teacher time. Wrong! No one can understand an assessment for a grade level like those teachers who are teaching in that grade level. So we allowed teachers to immediately review and make adjustments in the formative assessments so that concern would not be ongoing for the rest of the year. If we had ignored the genuine concerns that were hidden in the frustration, we would have not moved forward as successfully with the Eight Steps because of poor assessments. Separate frustration from true concerns. Action to resolve those concerns demonstrates that you, as a leader, are listening and willing to make adjustments. What I was not willing to compromise was whether we were going to go forward in implementing the Eight Steps.

Pat Davenport told me that the best thing about implementing a change is the first year only happens one time. She meant that once you survive the first year, and the second year is what they did the year before, most of the resistance melts.

Change is uncomfortable. It is personal. It is hard. It is easier to drift back into adult comfort behaviors that sabotage the change solution. Do not be too sympathetic to the difficulty of change. Otherwise, you will drift back to the status quo. The burden of proof is on those defending ineffective practices.

Scenarios

1. Use current disaggregated test data to create the picture of effectiveness. As you present the information, how will you engage teachers in making notes and observations during the analysis? How will you let the data become a mirror, reflecting an honest picture?

2. Classroom data for a teacher reflects a picture of low student achievement when compared to their achievement one year ago. The teacher blames the poverty, lack of parental support, and student mobility. Model how you will engage the teacher in focusing on her teaching effectiveness.

3. As you discuss formative assessment data with teachers, one teacher has the lowest scores in the grade level. Role play how you will approach that conversation, confronting the data but working toward an outcome that will encourage the teacher to participate in professional development to learn more effective strategies.

4. As you examine formative assessment data and grades for a particular student, there is a disconnect. What other data would you want to have before you begin the conversation?

CHAPTER THREE

THE "OPRAH" MOMENT: IT IS ALWAYS ABOUT RELATIONSHIPS AND INFLUENCE

ELCC Building and District Level Standards: 1.2, 1.3, 1.4, 2.1, 3.1

IF we are to influence educators about a change solution, we must first have some basis to develop the conversation about the effort. That basis is always the relationship with the individual. Fullan (2001) says "if moral purpose is job one, relationships are job two…"(p. 51). We frequently assume that the job responsibilities automatically give us a relationship with someone. It does, but not one of enough depth that can influence the individual's practice. We must notice their good work in the classroom or in the administrative role with important details that lets the individual know "we get it." Most people want to know that you care about them beyond just the job. Remaining in the professional context but paying attention to appropriate details of life can help build that relationship. Acknowledging efforts that go above and beyond whether at school or at their church, being empathetic to dealing with aging parents, asking about sick children, or just noticing a new haircut or their professional dress may seem trivial. But it is an acknowledgment that you are noticing them beyond their professional responsibilities. These acknowledgments typically occur as you make your rounds prior to school and you see individuals outside their classroom ready to welcome their students. When you take interest in a person, it communicates approval. We all want to be accepted.

In their book, *Encouraging the heart: A leader's guide to rewarding and recognizing others (1998),* Kouzes and Posner made the observation that "leaders create relationships" (p.xv). They describe seven essentials to developing relationships (p. 18):

• Setting clear expectations

• Expecting the best

• Paying attention

• Personalizing recognition

• Telling the story

• Celebrating together

• Setting the example

As we look to build relationships using these essentials, we find success because others know what they need to do to meet our expectations. And when we treat others as if they are effective teachers and leaders, most rise to that challenge.

In his later book, *The Six Secrets of Change (2008),* Fullan goes on to explain why loving your employees (Secret One in his book), is not enough.

Secret One, then, is not just about caring for employees. It is also about what works to get results. It is about sound strategies linked to impressive outcomes. One of the ways you love your employees is by creating the conditions for them to succeed....It is helping all employees find meaning, increased skill development, and personal satisfaction in making contributions that simultaneously fulfill their own goals and the goals of the organization.... (p. 25)

Visiting Classrooms

When I first began as a superintendent, I decided the only way to run a learning organization was to visit classrooms regularly. It gave me the opportunity to learn more about their daily teaching activities and they knew, by my attention to their work, that I valued that work. Memos do not communicate value. Words at a faculty meeting have a limited impact on communicating value. It takes the hard work of spending time where the learning is occurring.

I have always believed in the power of personal notes. When you take the time to jot a note to a teacher or administrator about their work, it means more than you can know. In education, we usually hear the negative. Or we hear very little about how we are doing. Positive notes, when appropriate, are rare. That is why educators keep them on their bulletin boards and computers as a reminder that someone values their work.

The desire to be appreciated by teachers by noticing their good work was brought back to reality for me when I announced my retirement as a superintendent after 28 years in three districts, and 38 years in public education. I was fortunate after the announcement to receive many positive messages from others. Two emails were important to this point of paying attention through notes to the good work of teachers. The first was an email from Bob Severs, a teacher at LaPorte High School in LaPorte, Indiana, where I served as superintendent from 1989-2001. He said, ""I always thought the world of you and kept every note you sent in my memory books. It's the little things that sometimes make the biggest impression." (Email from Bob Severs dated March 21, 2012) Another note came from Anna Stumpf, a former teacher at Walker Career Center for one year. "I still have the pad of paper with the note you left me that day…I have kept this in my desk since the day I received it…" (Email from Anna Stumpf dated April 9, 2012) (**Figure 3.1**) Is there any doubt left in your mind that personal notes make an impact? Visiting classrooms and noticing the good work of teachers and principals through personal notes builds relationships and tells them you are paying attention to the hard work of systemic change.

But this is not just about warm and fuzzy notes. When I observed teaching that caused concern, I shared that with the principal first and volunteered to speak with the teacher, leave the note in their mailbox as is, or allow the principal to share the note with them. My informal visits built relationships that allowed me to implement the Eight Step Process. If teachers had never seen me, as the superintendent, in their classrooms, they would have vented that I did not understand their classroom challenges. But because I had visited many classrooms and met with staff about their student data, we had some basis for a relationship.

Central office administrators with job responsibilities for curriculum

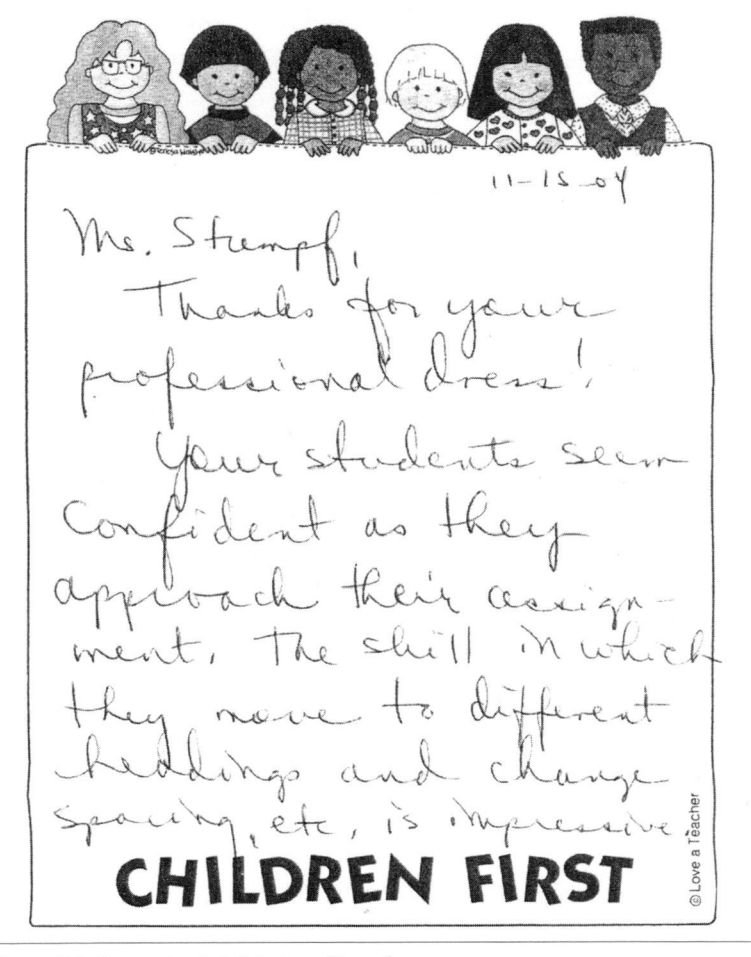

Figure 3.1 Personal note left to Anna Stumpf

and instruction should visit classrooms regularly. Visibility by those in the central office is key to building their relationship with principals as well as with teachers. It is also a critical step in monitoring school improvement efforts in schools to identify issues and problem solve solutions. Just being in the building as a central office administrator communicates the importance of the change initiative. But without visibility in the building on a regular basis, in classrooms, central office administrators cannot build a meaningful relationship with their principals and teachers as partners in the change process. There is a larger role for a central office person beyond compliance. Just being there in the building on a regular basis builds a vital relationship with that principal to assist with the issues about the change initiative that are unique to their building. It also builds credibility with teachers in your relationship with them because they see you actively engaged in the hard work of the change effort.

An important relationship is what occurs between the principal and teachers as well as among teachers.

Classroom Walkthroughs

Walkthroughs are quick visits by the principal to the classroom of about five minutes, focused on standards or the objective being taught, pacing of the lesson, review of the instructional materials being given to students, engagement of those students, effective teaching strategies, and classroom management. There is tremendous variation of this administrative strategy, including whether it is used for evaluation or not.

In Warren, we began with walkthroughs as monitoring efforts to ensure teachers were using our instructional calendars, a part of the Eight Step Process. They were not evaluative. With the changes in Indiana law, requiring yearly evaluations on every staff member, we decided to change walkthroughs to an evaluative strategy. **Figure 3.2** shows an elementary example of a walkthrough form while **Figure 3.3** illustrates a form used in middle school.

Warren principals provide their classroom walkthrough notes to teachers in addition to asking reflective questions to further the thinking of the teacher. When the purpose of walkthroughs are not well established and little feedback is received by the teacher, they see it as a "gotcha" rather than a tool for improvement. Technology has really enhanced the ability to share that feedback as the principal sends the information to the teacher's inbox as he/she walks out of the door. After a visit by anyone, teachers wonder what they are thinking. They are concerned about whether they did a good job or left a positive impression. Providing that feedback quickly reassures the teacher or, in the case of feedback that notes areas needing improvement, helps the teacher focus on improvement.

Hawthorne Elementary School
Classroom Walk-thru

Teacher _____ Date _____ Calendar _____ Time _____

Standard _____

Effective Lesson Area

___ Anticipatory Set   "activating prior knowledge"

___ State the Objective "what, how, why"

___ Teach Concepts and Skills "model", "break down concepts"

___ Check for Understanding "I do, we do, you do"

___ Provided Guided Practice "lead students in skill practice"

___ Independent Practice "practice of new knowledge"

___ Lesson Closure "review & summarize how / why"

Instructional Strategies / Materials

Higher Level Thinking / Engagement

L e v e l n f	Student Think	Student Think & Work
B l o o m ' s	Teacher Work	Student Work

Quantitative Data

____ # of students attending to the task

____ # of teacher questions

____ # of student questions

____ Use of proximity

____ Use of wait time (3-5 seconds)

.... Other _____

A p p l i c a t i o n

Level of Engagement

__ Persistence (problem solving, overcoming a challenge)   __ Differentiated (appropriate participation)

__ Symbolic (drama, drawing, etc.)   __ Focused Attention (watching or listening)

__ Encoded (appropriate interactive communication)   __ Undifferentiated (repetitive, low level)

__ Constructive (creating, making, building)   __ Casual Attention (wide ranging attention)

__ Non-Engagement (unoccupied behavior)

Evidence of Learning / Student Product / Learning Process

_____

_____

Reflective Feedback

_____

_____

_____

Figures 3.2 Walkthrough form

Administrators have the professional responsibility to do a certain number of observations, including classroom walkthroughs, to complete a teacher evaluation. Asking a reflective question as a part of those observations can promote an effective technique to initiate self-evaluation. Some of those reflective questions might be as follows:

• *Rather than relying on a paper and pencil activity, how might you have conducted this lesson to use more engaging techniques?*

• *In charting student responses, I noted only four students contributed something to the discussion. How might you have involved more students in making contributions?*

• *I noticed four students with their heads on the desk. As you walked around, how might you have intervened with these students without distracting others from the work?*

• *In reviewing the worksheet in which students were completing, the content appeared to be below grade level expectations. Help me to understand how the worksheet is connected to the grade level standards.*

• *As I look at your room, there are no artifacts of student work. Let's talk about how displaying student work contributes to the learning environment.*

Reflective practice, requiring the individual to think about their work and consider improvements, is a research proven tool that improves educator effectiveness. In building relationships, the reflective prompt promotes understanding, knowledge building, and builds capacity between the principal and teacher rather than just telling a teacher that their instructional effectiveness is limited. Our ultimate goal in using walkthroughs and other evaluative tools is to improve teacher effectiveness in producing student results.

Classroom walkthroughs are one way the building administrator pays attention to the important classroom work of teachers and provides helpful feedback on effectiveness or problem solves ways the teacher can improve. For most cases, it is conducted in the spirit of improvement.

Learning Log or Data Meetings

As mentioned previously, a continuous improvement district has a continuous data stream. In Warren, using the Eight Steps, our source of data was the three week formative assessments that measured the three week calendar window standards to determine the level of mastery by the students. This data was compiled by teachers in a grade level or content area to reflect mastery, partial mastery, or non-mastery. Using a modified Excel spreadsheet that highlights mastery in green, partial mastery in yellow, and non-mastery in red (**Figure 3.4**), teachers arrive at the learning log meeting with data already entered into the spreadsheet. The principal, who leads the meeting,

RPMS Classroom Walkthrough Feedback

Teacher _____   Date _____   Class/Period _____

Posted Standards Y N	Posted Objectives Y N	On Target Y N
Instructional Strategy:		
Taxonomy:	Key Words/Activities:	
Engaged/Off Task	Engagement Level of Engaged Students: ☐ ☐ ☐ ☐ ☐ ☐ Authentic ———————————— Ritualistic ——————————Passive	
Reflective Feedback		★

Reflective feedback questions may be answered in person as the opportunity allows or in a short, 2-5 sentence email.

Levels of Engagement

1. **Authentic Engagement**
   The type of engagement that occurs when the task, activity, or work the student is assigned is associated with a result that has clear meaning and immediate value to the student. (Reading a book on a sport or hobby that is of interest to the student)

2. **Ritual Engagement**
   The kind of engagement that occurs when the assigned work has little or no inherent meaning or immediate value to the student, but the student associates it with extrinsic results that are of value. (Reading a book in order to get a good grade on the test to qualify for college)

3. **Passive Compliance**
   The kind of engagement where the student is willing to expend whatever effort is necessary to avoid negative consequences, even though the student sees little meaning or value in the task. (Completing the homework assignment in order to avoid being "grounded" on the weekend)

4. **Retreatism**
   The student is disengaged from the task, expends little or no energy attempting to comply with the demands of the task or the teacher, but does not act in ways that disrupt others; does not try to substitute other activities for the assigned task.

5. **Rebellion**
   The student summarily refuses to do the tasks assigned; acts in ways that disrupt others, and/or tries to substitute tasks and activities to which the student is committed in lieu of those assigned or supported by the school and by the teacher.

Figures 3.3 Walkthrough form

displays all data for all teachers for the standards in the window.

In the beginning, the display of all student success or lack of it by all teachers in a grade or content area is intimidating. The purpose of looking at the data during the grade level meeting is to stimulate discussion about the organization of the Success Period, a daily 30 minute period devoted to reteaching non-mastery students or enriching

Eastridge   Learning Logs   4A   2011-12

Fourth Grade
Math

Teacher	# in class	Standard	Mastery		Partial		Non-Mastery		Mastery/Partial Combined	
	26	4.1.8	16	62%	8	31%	2	8%	24	92%
		4.1.9	14	54%	8	31%	4	15%	22	85%
		4.6.1	18	69%	7	27%	1	4%	25	96%
		4.6.2	21	81%	5	19%		0%	26	100%
		4.2.9		0%		0%		0%	0	0%
	26	4.1.8	18	69%	3	12%	3	12%	21	81%
		4.1.9	17	65%	4	15%	3	12%	21	81%
		4.6.1	9	35%	15	58%		0%	24	92%
		4.6.2	15	58%	7	27%	2	8%	22	85%
		4.2.9		0%		0%		0%	0	0%
	26	4.1.8	6	23%	16	62%	3	12%	22	85%
		4.1.9	13	50%	8	31%	5	19%	21	81%
		4.6.1	23	88%	2	8%	1	4%	25	96%
		4.6.2	15	58%	9	35%	2	8%	24	92%
		4.2.9		0%		0%		0%	0	0%
	24	4.1.8	6	25%	6	25%	12	50%	12	50%
		4.1.9	7	29%	10	42%	7	29%	17	71%
		4.6.1	19	79%	5	21%		0%	24	100%
		4.6.2	18	75%	3	13%	3	13%	21	88%
		4.2.9		0%		0%		0%	0	0%
E		4.1.8	#DIV/0!		#DIV/0!		#DIV/0!		0	#DIV/0!
		4.1.9	#DIV/0!		#DIV/0!		#DIV/0!		0	#DIV/0!
		4.6.1	#DIV/0!		#DIV/0!		#DIV/0!		0	#DIV/0!
		4.6.2	#DIV/0!		#DIV/0!		#DIV/0!		0	#DIV/0!
		4.2.9	#DIV/0!		#DIV/0!		#DIV/0!		0	#DIV/0!
TALLY	102	4.1.8	46	45%	33	32%	20	20%	79	77%
	102	4.1.9	51	50%	30	29%	19	19%	81	79%
	102	4.6.1	69	68%	29	28%	2	2%	98	96%
	102	4.6.2	69	68%	24	24%	7	7%	93	91%
	0	4.2.9	0	#DIV/0!	0	#DIV/0!	0	#DIV/0!	0	#DIV/0!

Figure 3.4 Learning Log Grade Level Data-Eastridge Elementary

mastery students. By collaborating across classrooms, teachers can regroup the grade level students by levels of mastery, identifying all available teachers (including special area teachers like art, music, and PE as well as special education teachers) and instructional assistants to teach those groups based on the data. In time, discussion moves into what effective strategies were used by certain teachers to reach higher levels of mastery (**Figures 3.5** and **3.6**) If you think about the traditional structure of school, when do teachers have an opportunity to share effective strategies based on student success data on a regular basis? The building of relationships among teachers and between the principal and teachers increases as they focus on instruction and work together to improve student outcomes.

Learning log meetings provide a forum for teachers to identify individual students who have experienced great progress or seem to have developed a downward pattern that may require counselor or administrator intervention. The best part of these discussions is a

MSD of WARREN TOWNSHIP
Grade-Level Team Meeting Questions

Share and discuss available test results, especially the 3-week assessments. Dissect the results by subgroups and individual students. Remember, **data drives instruction!!**

Are there any noticeable patterns?

What percentage of students mastered each skill/indicator?

What instructional diagnosis can you make? What approach/intervention was used? Should a different approach be used?

Based on student performance, will you need to revise time allocations for teaching a skill or indicator?

For those who were successful, have they really learned the skill or were they lucky?

How did the "partial mastery" students do? Remember, if these students are not 'getting it,' there could be something amiss in the delivery of the instruction or the test item for that skill.

What maintenance strategies are we going to use?

Figure 3.5 Grade Level team Meeting Questions and Team Learning Log

concept developed at Raymond Park Middle School known as the Guarantee Board (**Figure 3.7**). Teachers select a student who has not passed the state assessment and, based on progress demonstrated during the year, guarantee the student will pass the state assessment. Teachers share this with the individual student. Imagine the impact of a teacher guaranteeing a student's success and communicating to that student the confidence the teacher has in him/her. In the first year of the Guarantee Board, 60% of students passed the state assessment after previous failures.

We have other data sources known as benchmarking data or progress monitoring. At risk students are progress monitored every two weeks, while students at other level of risk are monitored less frequently. We use DIBELS, TRC, mClass, DRA, and Acuity. The progress monitoring data is displayed in a data wall (**Figure 3.8**) in

TEAM LEARNING LOG

GRADE LEVEL: _____   **DATE:** _____

PRESENT:
- ☐ Grade level team
- ☐ Principal
- ☐ Dean
- ☐ Coach
- ☐ Interventionalist
- ☐ Other_____

Targeted Indicator(s)/Area of Weakness from Formative Assessments:
(What Data did you use? Why did you choose this indicator?)

_____

_____

_____

Evaluation of Instructional Solutions: (Specifically, what must students know and be able to do? What steps are required?)

_____

_____

_____

Instructional Solutions to Address Above Weakness: (What strategies will you use? How will you integrate higher level thinking activities? How will you integrate real world application?)

For Success Period: (Who will teach enrichment, re-teaching, and remediation? What skills will be targeted? What materials will you use?)

_____

_____

_____

_____

_____

For Tier II: (Who will teach? What Skills? What Materials?)

_____

_____

_____

_____

_____

Assessments used to appraise growth after targeted instruction:
- ☐ Form B
- ☐ Summative
- ☐ Core Programs
- ☐ Voyager
- ☐ Acuity
- ☐ TRC
- ☐ DIBELS
- ☐ Student Conferencing
- ☐ Anecdotal Notes
- ☐ Daily Work
- ☐ Teacher Observation

Figure 3.6 Grade Level team Meeting Questions and Team Learning Log

secure teacher areas for discussion during data meetings. Teachers are looking for inconsistencies between three week assessment data and progress monitoring data as well as predictive data that indicates progress toward passing the state assessment. Today we have many sources of data. Our focus must be keeping track of it, making certain

Anticipated Short-Term Results within next 3 Week Window: (percentage of mastery of targeted indicator)

_____

_____

_____

Adjustments to Instruction (What will be the next steps if results are not satisfactory?)

_____

_____

_____

Which students will you specifically target for improvement?

_____   _____

_____   _____

What strategies are in place that support improvement in your targeted AYP cells:

_____

_____

Are students involved in GEI/CCEIS (Comprehensive Coordinated Early Intervening Services)?

_____   _____

_____   _____

Are any students being consider for retention:

_____   _____

_____   _____

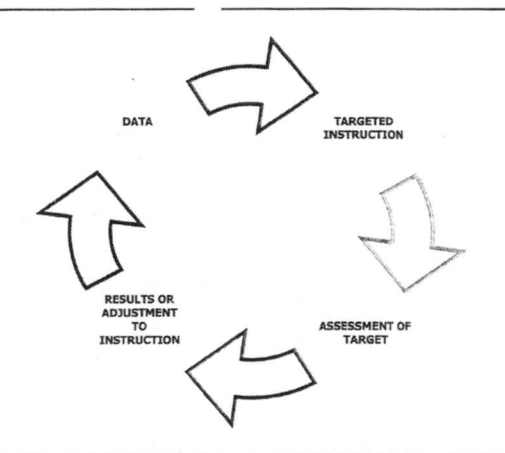

Figure 3.6 Grade Level team Meeting Questions and Team Learning Log

data drives teaching decisions, and keeping the data wall up to date so it portrays visually our learning focus. As student benchmarking data is reviewed, each "sticky note" which represents a student is moved up or down into the levels. Once again, colors are used to

Figure 3.7 Guarantee Board

identify Pass Plus (upper 10%) with blue, green is mastery, yellow are "bubble kids" who are just above or below the mastery level, and red is a non-mastery student.

We also use this data to discuss Response to Intervention, creating Tier 2 and 3 groups who need additional instruction to succeed

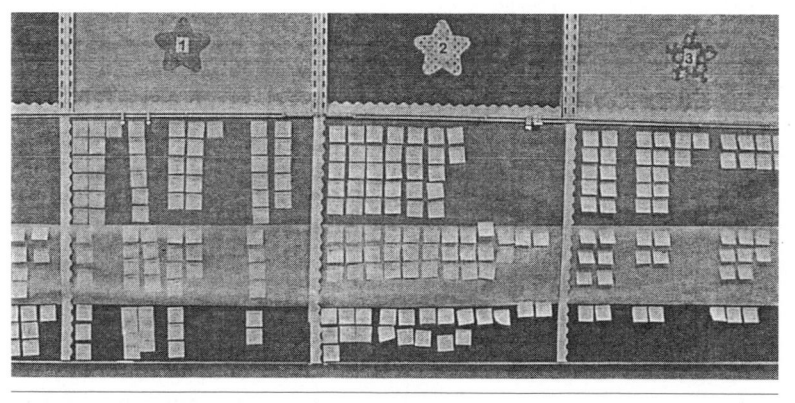

Figure 3.8 Data Wall

Figure 3.9 Sample schedule for Tier 2 and 3 instruction

(**Figure 3.9**). Once students participate in the daily 30 minute Success Period, they may need these additional interventions.

What a powerful relationship among teachers as they use data not to criticize efforts but to make teaching decisions! In isolation, teachers cannot manage four daily groups representing reteaching in language arts and math and enriching in the same content areas. By working as a grade or content area, they can reorganize their students to address their needs. Teacher teams operate like well-oiled machines, sharing professional strategies and problem solving the issues uncovered by the data. There is a high level of trust. Note that not all teacher teams are high functioning. Over time, teachers are very good are determining with whom they can work effectively and principals engage teachers in those conversations to strengthen the grade level teams for maximum effectiveness. Now accountability has a different feel because the learning organization is focused on placing teachers on teams where they can be most effective.

As these techniques demonstrate, building strong relationships between teachers and administrators and among teachers builds influence. When you trust a colleague, you listen to their ideas, allowing their influence to contribute to a better solution. These relationships are also key to the implementation of the change solution. The monitor and adjust portion of the change solution takes place through these relationship vehicles.

Scenarios

1. You visit a classroom and observe students quietly working on a worksheet at their desk. The class is orderly. The teacher is sitting at his/her desk, grading papers. Her student achievement results are typically very good. How do you begin the conversation about improvement, noting engagement and monitoring, among other issues?

2. During a walkthrough, you notice that a classroom has several unruly students, standing on the low bookcases and one child wandering the classroom. As you see this, how will you react? Model the conversation with the teacher at his/her next free period.

3. As you conduct learning log meetings to review the data for each teacher and student on specific standards, you see a pattern of low achievement for one teacher in every three week period. The teacher appears to be unconcerned about her data. The three week data is formative in nature, giving the team information on the levels of mastery. Thus, it is not evaluative in nature. However, it indicates a weakness in instructional strategies. As you use the data as a mirror in a private conversation with the teacher, what questions will you ask to increase her level of concern?

4. A grade level team of teachers is dysfunctional with too much drama. Individual teachers lack trust in each other's ability to teach their students, creating conflict over the organization of instruction for reteaching and enriching standards. They barely speak during the grade level team meeting. What specific actions will you take to work through their issues and help them build a more collaborative relationship?

CHAPTER FOUR

TEACHER LEADERSHIP, THE SECRET INGREDIENT

ELCC Building and District Level Standards: 1.3, 1.4, 2.2, 2.3, 2.4, 3.1, 3.2, 3.3

TEACHER leadership is critical to any high performing school. Katzenmeyer and Moller (2001) provide this definition of teacher leadership: "*Teachers who are leaders lead within and beyond the classroom, identify with and contribute to a community of teacher learners and leaders, and influence others toward improved educational practice.*" *(p.5)* The authors emphasize that the key in teacher leadership is influence, expanding our thinking beyond the individual classroom and into the collective capacity of all teachers within a building.

When we look at the research on the power of teachers, Hattie (2009) defines elements that have above average effects on student achievement as "*teachers using particular teaching methods, teachers with high expectations for all students, and teachers who have created positive student-teacher relationships...*" *(p.126)* University preparation may lack focus on the development of these elements or veteran teachers may have dated skills. The leadership challenge is building teacher leaders who can build these skills sets among teachers and influence their professional practice.

Changing the Culture of Autonomy to a Culture of Teams

As I reflect upon my first year of teaching, I felt like I had rented a space in a flea market where I shut the door and did whatever

I thought was best for my students. As a first year teacher, the assumption from my principal was I knew what to do. I never had an observation by my principal until November of that first year. As I reflect on my teaching years, I realize that there was no consistency in our approach to teaching. What students learned, or did not learn, would vary from teacher to teacher, depending on their emphasis in the curriculum taught and their effectiveness in doing so. Advice from other teachers was "on the fly" as we ate lunch or had coffee in the morning. There was no systematic focus on developing effective teaching methods, learning how to operationalize high expectations for all students, and creating positive teacher-student relationships. It was trial by fire and survival of the fittest.

Building a culture of teaming among a grade or content level takes intentional strategies. It begins with building teams that have collaborative working relationships which requires some trial and error.

I can think of two examples where efforts to build collaborative teacher teams faltered. We had one teacher who did not want to regroup all students in the grade level for Success Period, which was a part of the Eight Step Process. She did not trust other teachers to do the same quality work as she believed she would do with her own students. She transferred to another building and eventually learned, once we set a district expectation that regrouping the grade level and sharing students was a professional expectation, to work with others.

Another situation involved a veteran teacher placed on a middle school team with all young teachers. She found their conversations about their social life, including more than she wanted to know about their world of dating and night life, to be offensive. Her life focused on her family and home. The dynamics of this mismatched team required the principal to make a change. The leadership from the veteran teacher in trying to focus on student achievement issues never rooted with the young teachers.

As teams begin with student data, it focuses the conversation on results, effective strategies, and interventions. Principals can use questions during these data meetings to keep teams focused, as shared in Figures 3.5 and 3.6. As teams work toward common goals, results improve. The interpersonal dynamics require all teachers to respect each other, listen to one another, not allow any one team member to dominate the conversation, and offer constructive criticism focused on making the necessary adjustments to improve results.

Coaching: The New Leadership Skill

The Association for Supervision and Curriculum Development's (ASCD) magazine, Educational Leadership, devoted its October, 2011 issue to the issue of coaching. The articles explore this new leadership relationship between and among teachers as they work as partners, learning and sharing effective instructional strategies. This instructional support for teachers by teachers is essential to expanding the role of the principal as instructional leader. In Cognitive Coaching (2002), Costa and Garmston frame important skill sets by coaches as not being judgmental, giving teachers time to reflect upon the coach's questions, and having a strategy in mind as they worked with a teacher. *"This focus is based on the belief that growth is achieved through the development of intellectual functioning. Therefore, the coaching interaction focuses on mediating a practitioner's thinking, perceptions, beliefs, and assumptions toward the goals of self-directed learning and increased complexity of cognitive processing." (p.5)* Warren has used instructional coaches since our involvement with Reading First, having found coaches to deliver effective professional development in the classroom. Traditional in-service programs provided no classroom support for a teacher when they returned to their classroom and attempted new teaching strategies. As a result, they abandoned the new effort. With coaches, teachers receive support from peers in their classroom with their students until they have mastered the new skill.

With budget cuts, many districts have eliminated coaching positions. Principals can identify effective teachers from student results and arrange visitations to those classrooms to observe effective strategies. Teachers can demonstrate strategies as a part of faculty meetings. When these coaches return to the classroom during tight budgets, principals must become resourceful in capturing their expertise in alternative ways.

Beginning the Journey of Discovery

If your school is not faring well under accountability, begin a conversation with teachers as you look at current achievement data. (This could also be used to look at discipline referrals, building procedures in hallways and classrooms, and suspension data.) Listen carefully to teacher frustrations with the current approach. Contribute observations from the building administration. List elements of a change solution that is important to all. Fullan (2001) reminds us of this important principle:

"Leadership, then, is not mobilizing others to solve problems we already know how to solve, but to help them confront problems that have never yet been successfully addressed." (p.3)

As we listen to what educators think are the root cause of our problems, conversations usually resort to the usual list of societal problems of poverty, single-parent families, lack of individual responsibility, etc., focusing on causes outside the influence of educators. When accountability uncovers the brutal truth of our lack of success, we must face our reality that what we have been doing is not working. It is tough to admit that what may have worked for 20 years in our classroom does not work today. But the sooner we face the truth, the sooner we can move on to solutions that work.

When these critical conversations are not held, change solutions are sometimes forced by district administrators. While this is not the best way to begin, it is important to note that usually "one school solutions" do not work. If there is an unsolved problem, it is probably present in the entire district, not just an individual school. Systemic change will produce lasting results and district solutions reduce variation in the system. When schools are resistant to confronting their problems, others may have to force solutions.

After about five years of implementing the Eight Step process in Warren, our elementary teachers, along with Assistant Superintendent Dena Cushenberry and elementary principals, looked at our student writing scores and found them to be resistant to improvement. They formed a writing cadre with representation from each school. They researched writing processes, selected Lucy Calkins' Writer's Workshop, went to training, began to implement in the classrooms of the writing cadre teachers, filmed their lessons, and prepared a two-hour in-service for opening day for all elementary teachers. (**Figure 4.1**) The only

Writer's Workshop

What is Writer's Workshop?

A framework for instruction, in which students move through the writing process at their own pace.

Writing Workshop - Components

- Mini-Lesson (10 - 20 minutes)
- Status of the Class (3 - 5 minutes)
- Work Time (25 – 30 minutes)
- Share Time (5 – 7 minutes)

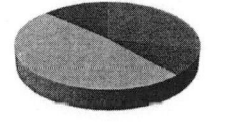

- ■ Mini Lesson
- ■ Status of Class
- ▨ Work Time
- ■ Share

What Makes the Writing Workshop Approach Successful?

- Explicit Instruction- Teachers model what good writers do each day. Students are directly taught specific skills and strategies to improve their writing daily.
- Choice! Even though students are working on the same unit of study, they have freedom to choose what to write about.
- Engagement- As a result of being able to choose what they write about, students are highly engaged in the process, and show ownership of their finished product.

Figure 4.1 Writer's Workshop

involvement they allowed me, the superintendent, was to ask for half of my opening day time for the in-service! Teacher leadership at its best!

Further, the dilemma was how to fit Writer's Workshop into the daily schedule. Writing cadre teachers looked at each elementary school schedule, determined that each school could find 45 minutes per day to implement the process, and set those expectations with teachers. (Figure 4.2) If I, as superintendent, had set that expectation, teachers would have resisted. But the power of teacher leadership in crafting a solution pays huge dividends when they are allowed to function as leaders. The result: improved student writing scores!

Non – Negotiable

90 Minute (Tier 1)	= 90 minutes
Tier 2	= 30 minutes
Tier 3	= 30 minutes
Math	= 30 minutes
Success (Math)	= 30 minutes
Lunch	= 30 minutes
Recess	= 20 minutes
Special Classes	= 40 minutes
Writer's Workshop	= 45 minutes
Total Time (approx.)	

5 hrs. 45 min.

School Day   7 hrs.
Non – negotiables   – 5.75 hrs
1 hr. 15 min.

Figure 4.2 Non-Negotiables

Learning Together Works Best

As the change solution is introduced by the district or the building administrator, the evidence of the need through data is usually presented with the logic of this change solution and how it will meet those needs. The training is then scheduled. It is absolutely critical that the administrators participate fully in the training as a learner if they are to be believed as the person in charge of monitoring the implementation. There are too many times when I have been a part of training as the trainer and watched the administrators give cursory attention to participation in the details as part of the learning journey with their teachers. They pay too much attention to their cell phones and Blackberry devices, leaving the training frequently to deal with something. It is sometimes valid. But sometimes it is an avoidance technique because learning something new takes effort.

Teachers are watching this behavior closely. The great teachers that take an idea and have it implemented the next day will do so anyway. But the group in the middle will determine the success of the change solution in your school. And they are watching the administrators to see if they are willing to learn this new, complex material in order to make the changes that will positively impact student achievement. When the administrators are present and active participants in the training, the training breaks create opportunities to have rich dialogue with teachers about what they have learned. Administrators can ask their teachers questions about how they see the necessary adjustments in their classroom routine to incorporate the change. They learn together. More importantly, when the administrator respects the work, he/she respects the teachers. The work becomes a collaborate process, not a dictated one from the administrator.

Strategic Movers and Shakers

Once administrators have participated with their teachers in the training, they need to assess and create with teachers the implementation or action plan. Teachers must have the opportunity to demonstrate leadership as these action plans are created. (**Figure 4.3**) Action plans focus on the gap between where we are and where we should be in our efforts. Those teacher leaders who have influence on other teachers are strategic to a successful implementation of a change solution.

As teachers develop the steps for the action plan for each element of the change solution, the challenge for the building administrator will be to allow them to lead the effort. Teacher leadership is imperative if there is to be ownership of the change solution. When the principal

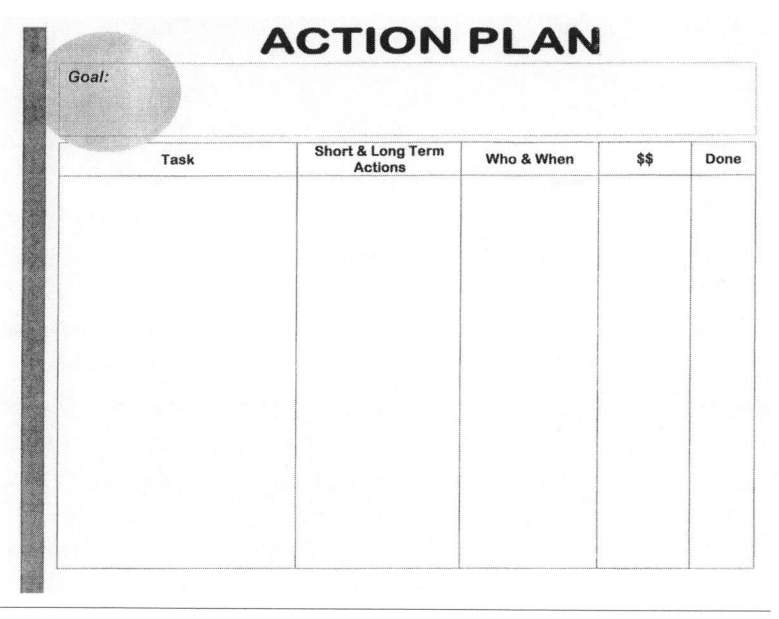

Figure 4.3 Action Plan

prepares the action plan and gives it to teachers, they have nothing vested in the proposed solution. So when it fails, and it will, they blame it on the principal. When teachers develop the action plan and they present it to teachers, they are a part of the solution. They will work to refine their solution, influence and support teachers who may be struggling, and quietly isolate the blockers. The administrator's role is to keep the focus and allow nothing to interfere. The relentless caring for the mission of the intended change solution will become the passion of those dedicated educators.

Data Walls

Teachers can monitor their effectiveness with data walls (See Chapter 3). Each swath of color connects teachers with student progress. The color banners are red for non-mastery students, yellow for "bubble" students who have either just passed the assessment or just missed the cut score for the assessment, green for mastery students, and blue for students who have achieved at the highest levels. Each sticky note represents a student. Other information such as whether the child is in special education, a child of color of ethnicity, a child of poverty, etc. may be noted with color coding or other methods. The data wall gives teachers a clear visual on student progress. These data walls are protected in conference areas where teachers meet but are not accessible to parents or students. Teachers move students up or down, depending on the latest benchmark data. These data walls are a vehicle for teachers to know student data for each child and be familiar with their progress, or lack of it. More importantly, the data wall is a vehicle for collaboration among teachers. They can determine additional Tier 2 or 3 interventions or recommend additional testing. No longer are decisions made by assumptions about learners. Now decisions are based on data.

Steve Foster, former principal at Lakeside Elementary School and now at Creston Intermediate Academy in Warren, decided to put student pictures on each sticky note. He wanted his teachers to understand that most of the non-mastery and "bubble" students were children of color. The visual the student pictures on the sticky notes created for staff made his point and raised awareness of their low achievement. His school made Adequate Yearly Progress for seven straight years, in spite of high levels of poverty and transiency.

Process Checks

Process checks are a way to conduct a "temperature check" on the implementation of the change solution. It involves listing each element of the change solution, asking teachers to reflect in writing on what has been accomplished and weaknesses in the implementation of each element, and engaging them with the principal in celebrating progress and problem solving remaining issues in the implementation.

Figure 4.4 was used in our process checks with the Eight Step Continuous Improvement Process over ten years in Warren. We engaged Pat Davenport to return to the district each year and conduct the process checks on site at each school campus. While principals were always in the process checks along with the superintendent and other central office staff, teachers carried the conversation about their successes and continued challenges. The level of collaboration and cooperation becomes evident in these process checks. Some

IDOE Eight Step Process Review

Step 1: Data Disaggregation

Success

_____
_____
_____
_____

Challenge

_____
_____
_____
_____

Step 2: Calendar Development

Success:_____
_____
_____
_____

Challenge:_____
_____
_____
___

Step 3: Instructional Focus

Success:_____
_____
_____
_____

Challenge:_____
_____
_____
_____

___
Step 4: Assessment

Success:_____
_____
_____

Challenge:_____

―

Step 5/6: Tutorials Enrichment

Success:_____

Challenge:_____

――

Step 7: Maintenance

Success:_____

Challenge:_____

―

Step 8: Monitoring

Success:_____

Challenge:_____

Figure 4.4 Process Check Form – Pat Davenport

teams have negative energy, signaling a need to move teachers into other grade levels to maximize their effectiveness. When teams demonstrate positive energy and enthusiasm, it is clear that nothing will stop them from achieving great goals on behalf of children. This is where teachers develop ownership of the work. Once they own the work, the implementation has rooted. But they will only develop ownership if they are allowed to make those incremental changes that tweak an implementation and make it more effective. Wise principals listen to their teachers and as long as the non-negotiables are not compromised, these adjustments improve the implementation plan.

Any change solution must make the case to teachers and teacher leaders, convincing them that the change will pass their test of common sense, addressing the needs of the students they serve. They must also see a glimmer of hope that the change solution the district is suggesting connects with their knowledge and background. While they may be worried about how the change solution will impact their daily teaching behaviors, most teachers will resonate to a change solution if they are a part of the consideration of the change solution.

Teachers are the secret ingredient in any change solution. Without their support, nothing will move forward. Whatever is implemented will be better if teachers have input into necessary adjustments.

Scenarios

1. The instructional coach provides a schedule of classroom visits. The principal notices that several teachers are consistently not on the schedule. When questioned, the coach indicates these teachers do not want her in their room. Model your conversation with the coach and the non-compliant teachers.

2. Teachers are quietly complaining about the instructional coach, indicating a lack of effectiveness. You observe the coach and believe the strategies modeled are appropriate. However, you sense a problem with interpersonal skills. How will you confront the coach and model more effective interpersonal interactions with the coach?

3. As principal, you want to move many teachers to different grade levels and teams. Construct the criteria by which you will make these decisions.

4. On a grade level team, one teacher consistently dominates the conversation. As you observe the team dynamics, you notice other teachers withdrawing. Model your critical conversation with the dominating teacher and with the other teachers on the team.

CHAPTER FIVE

MONITORING: TROUBLESHOOTING, PROBLEM SOLVING, AND PAYING CLOSE ATTENTION

ELCC Building and District Standards: 1.3, 1.4, 2.2, 2.3, 3.1, 3.2

LEADERS sometimes believe just because they say it, educators will follow. Leaders must monitor the change by establishing the non-negotiables of the effort, observing and discussing these non-negotiables to determine compliance, checking for transfer of the learning of the training to the classroom, and checking for the consistency of classroom implementation within the school. This is the step frequently ignored that becomes the root cause to the downfall of the change effort. Monitoring is not only the responsibility of the building leaders but also the district leaders. They must confront problems with solutions, involving educators. They must confront those who are not compliant with the established non-negotiable elements of the change and have the difficult conversations. Without this step, the leader is doomed to fail.

Now that you have visited classrooms, engaged teachers about conclusions drawn from their data, and listened to teacher feedback, an administrator begins to identify implementation issues that require further discussion. These problems should be seen as the natural result of any change effort that requires new behaviors from educators. The pull of past practices, routines, and adult comforts will always cloud the implementation plan. The purpose of monitoring is to identify those issues, work through solutions, and further monitor for understanding and compliance.

The first step to understanding the depth of the implementation by individual teachers lies in setting expectations for what you expect to see in the classroom, known as the "non-negotiables." These expectations should be a part of the training for the change solution and in writing in documents that are continually discussed in teacher meetings.

When we began the implementation of the Eight Steps Continuous Improvement Process, we defined **four non-negotiables: calendars, three week assessments, the daily 30 minute Success Period, and the learning log meetings.** I reinforced these non-negotiables every opening day with staff at the start of the school year, it was in our school improvement documents, and principals reinforced the non-negotiables in their exchanges with teachers. We left little to chance about what we expected to see in the implementation of Eight Steps. When we saw evidence of straying from those non-negotiables, it provided a context for a conversation about expectations, clarifying any misunderstandings, and moving forward with fidelity of the implementation.

Troubleshooting

Once you have identified deviations from those expectations, it is your responsibility to engage the educator about the root cause. I have learned the hard way not to assume I know why variations have occurred or to assume the person is resisting the effort. I have found it best to begin with one of two important phrases…

"Tell me about _____"

"Help me to understand_____"

These phrases allow you to "wade into the conversation" with safety.

The authors of *Crucial Conversations: Tools for talking when stakes are high (2002),* define a crucial conversation as "a discussion between two or more people where (1) stakes are high, (2) opinions vary, and (3) emotions run strong." (p.3) The book defines how to face these conversations and handle them well. As I noted earlier, the need for these conversations arises out of the natural progression of the change solution, not because the teacher is bad or does not care about improving. The stakes of accountability are high. A teacher may believe the administrator does not understand what he/she is doing instructionally in the classroom and questioning an educator about his/her practice invokes a sense of outrage because the educator believes he/she is doing just fine. Troubleshooting requires the critical conversation with the teacher about his/her practice while building your relationship in the process. If confronting the issue diminishes the relationship, everyone loses. When we realize it is time to confront an issue, we can get mad and scold, mumble about it under our breath, or effectively confront it without damaging the relationship.

The authors describe the following process to begin these crucial conversations:

1. *Start with Heart. Begin high risk discussions with the right motives and they will stay focused. Focus on what you really want to result from the conversation.*

2. *Remain honest and respectful to the individual, no matter how they respond to the conversation. Keep them focused on what you want for students. (pp.30-31)*

Some might refer to it as "just the facts" as you stay focused on what is in the best interests of the children. What do we want to see, what do we see, what is the gap, and what are the possible solutions?

An example of such a conversation that confronts a practice, influences a new behavior, and builds the relationship is illustrated by Principal Ryan Russell of Raymond Park Intermediate Academy in Warren Township. After disseminating an outline of clear expectations to all teachers, Ryan conducts his classroom visits. He notices in the classroom of Jen Hess, an accomplished teacher, that her higher achieving students were tuning out. In sharing that feedback with her, she made an immediate adjustment in her classroom plan to allow those students to meet as a group on their own. This allowed their discussion to reach a higher level. (This story was reported in the *Indianapolis Star* on March 11, 2012.) Rather than take this feedback as criticism, Mrs. Hess made an adjustment and felt better about her ability to challenge those students. Her relationship with her principal remained trustworthy and viable because he gave her the feedback, knowing that she would determine a better response with just a question from him because of her effectiveness as a teacher.

These conversations do not always go well. I can remember in the early years of implementing Eight Steps we had a few teachers that did not trust their children to another teacher to remediate. They told the principal they did not want to participate in the collaboration with other teachers and were doing just fine on their own. The principal had a conversation something like this:

"Mrs. Smith, I know you have been a dedicated teacher for many years. I am grateful for your dedication. Can you share with me why you do not want to participate in the learning log meetings with your other grade level teachers?"

"I feel I am a better teacher than the others because of my years of experience. I don't trust other people to get my job done in helping the challenging students."

"You are aware of the district expectation of non-negotiables that includes your participation in learning log meetings and collaboration in planning the daily Success Period. This has been taken to discussion with the teachers' union and everyone understands this is our professional obligation. How can I help you comply with our district expectations?"

"You mean I don't have a choice? What happened to academic freedom?"

"Our superintendent has been clear and I know you would not want to be viewed as insubordinate. You have had an exemplary career here and I know you have so much to offer to those less experienced teachers."

"Honestly, it is easier to do it within my own classroom. All this regrouping of students every three weeks is a lot of work."

"Yes, it is. But if you think about it, every day we are providing remediation and enrichment to our students based on their scores on the three week assessments. Could you manage that in your classroom?"

"No, I cannot. I guess I have to do this."

"I would rather that you look at it as helping our grade level teachers use effective strategies to get better results with our students. You can be a leader among our staff in this way. Can I count on you?"

"Yes, I guess. But what if I don't do it right?"

"I will be here to help you. Trust your great instincts as a teacher. They have served you well for many years."

In this conversation that began with identifying her noncompliance to the non-negotiables, he made it safe by acknowledging her past effectiveness. He then clarified expectations and connected to her desire to help other teachers. He continued to build his relationship with her by reassuring her he would be there to support her as she began to learn these new behaviors. He not only pulled her back into compliance, but did so without damaging their relationship,

Continuous Improvement Tools

There are continuous improvement tools that will help you work through implementation issues. Chang and Niedzwiecki (1993) have two volumes describing these tools. Here is a sample of the most common ones:

- **Brainstorming (pgs. 5-13):** *generate as many ideas as possible without criticism; quantity of ideas, including "piggybacking" on the idea of another*

- **Affinity Diagram (pgs. 15-23):** *state the problem, use cards or sticky notes and have participants write one idea on each card or note, arrange notes in related groups, prioritize*

- **Cause and Effect (also known as root cause analysis – pgs. 47-57):** *identify the effect, identify major causes, ask why until you reach the root cause*

These and other quality tools can assist educators with monitoring efforts.

Teachers as Change Agents

These crucial conversations are not limited to interactions between the principal and teacher. Teachers can hold these conversations as they work through the implications of student data and what needs to be done.

"In this three week period, we need more remediation groups than enrichment groups. That will mean that all of the classroom teachers will have Success groups, remediating this math standard."

"But I am more effective with enrichment students. Let one of the instructional assistants handle the extra remediation group."

"As classroom teachers, we are highly trained to conduct remediation groups. Instructional assistants have minimal training. As teachers, we need for you to step up and conduct this remediation class. You are an accomplished teacher. We will be happy to share some of our remediation strategies. We are confident you can do the job."

"If you are willing to help me, I am willing to try."

Once again, they confronted the attempt to return to adult comfort zones without damaging the relationship. They kept it safe by addressing her expertise and offered support in sharing effective strategies. These teachers successfully held a crucial conversation on their own.

Initial Implementation Issues

In my 28 years as a superintendent engaged in various school improvement efforts, most recently Eight Steps, it has been my observation that monitoring the school improvement process is usually the forgotten step. As Pat Davenport has trained us in Warren and over 130 schools in Indiana in the Eight Steps, Step 8 is monitoring, or checking how well the process is being implemented. Districts implement a program or process, provide professional development, and assume the implementation will proceed as trained. It rarely does.

Heifetz and Linsky (2002) write about the dangers of adaptive change. They differentiate technical problems, those for which people can apply current knowledge to solve, from adaptive challenges, learning new ways which require experimentation and discovery. (p.13) They offer this caution:

In mobilizing adaptive work, you have to engage people in adjusting their unrealistic expectations, rather than try to satisfy them as if the situation were amenable primarily to a technical remedy. You have to counteract their exaggerated dependency and promote their resourcefulness. This takes an extraordinary level of presence, time, and artful communication, but it may also take more time and trust than you have. (p.15)

So why does implementation experience flaws? Here are a few reasons:

- *"I don't remember the training saying we had to do this?" (Code: I don't want to do this because I might fail.)*
- *"This new program/process will require me to stop doing what has worked for years." (Code: I don't want to expend the energy to change what is comfortable for me.)*
- *"Until parents step up, nothing will change so why try?" (Code: The lack of achievement is not my fault. I could do better if parents sent us better students.)*

And so on...

What needs to change in the dynamics of school improvement efforts to produce more long lasting effects? In Pat Davenport's work in implementing the Eight Steps in schools on the state takeover list, five high schools made significant improvement, enough to "get off the list." How did she accomplish that? She monitored the implementation on site every month against the plan, identified variations, made connections, and guided staff back on track. Her effectiveness came from the relationship she had built with them in the training and subsequent visits. Sometimes she listened with empathy. Other times she scolded them for less than a robust effort, especially given the current student achievement levels. That reality check, although sometimes brutal, kept people on track with the school improvement effort.

In my eleven years at Warren, we worked with teachers and administrators to implement Eight Steps. Principals monitored along with central office staff who attended process checks during the year as well as learning log meetings and Success Period. Pat Davenport conducted third party process checks with principals, teachers and district administrators each year for a decade.

Instructional Coaches

One of the most exciting developments in the last decade has been the proliferation of instructional coaches. These are teachers who provide professional development in the classroom for teachers on proven practices. Their emergence began as a part of the federal Reading First program. Schools in improvement had to include literacy coaches as a part of their improvement plan.

When the idea of literacy coaches was first discussed with me as a superintendent, I did not believe teachers would accept the help from another teacher. I remember thinking that the coaches would be thrown out of those classrooms. I also assumed that the teachers' union would oppose teachers in staff development roles whom remained in their bargaining unit. How wrong I was!

When the most effective instructional coach is selected because of their proven expertise and respect from other teachers, they provide a critical role that is lacking in most change solutions. After the initial training, when teachers go back into the classroom to attempt new teaching behaviors, they may struggle. Who is there to help them? The trainer is on to the next job. The already overwhelmed administrator has limited time to model the teaching behavior with the advent of yearly teacher evaluations and other reform demands. The instructional coach can model the teaching strategy in that teacher's own classroom which is critical to dealing with his/her situation. The coach then returns to observe the teacher trying the strategy, providing feedback to the teacher in a non-evaluative way, and reteaching any portion of the strategy that remains challenging to the teacher. These coaches focus on mastery of the new teaching behaviors, not evaluating the same teachers. Their key leadership role allows the change solution to move forward by building relationships and teacher competencies, not by expectations without support. Further, coaches serve in a monitoring role in ensuring the non-negotiable elements are being implemented.

Monitoring requires paying close attention to the details of the change solution, identifying variations from those expectations that threaten the fidelity of that implementation, and problem solving with individuals the way back to the implementation plan.

Scenarios

1. Teachers identify an issue with high numbers of students in remediation groups. Model how you will use brainstorming to determine a solution to the high numbers.

2. As you monitor for compliance to the elements of your change effort, you discover an entire grade level (or content area) is not implementing a key element. How will you determine the scope of non-compliance? Model the conversation with the teachers, including how you will reset expectations and monitor compliance.

3. Create your personal plan for monitoring your change effort. How will you ensure its implementation, short of emergencies?

4. Even though your change effort requires the regrouping of all students in a grade level, you discover a grade level that has drifted back to adult comfort levels and is not regrouping. Once you confront them, the teachers say it is too time consuming. What will you say next?

CHAPTER SIX

WHEN TROUBLE PERSISTS: HAVING THE DIFFICULT CONVERSATIONS

ELCC Building and District Level Standards: 1.3, 2.2, 2.3, 2.4, 3.1, 3.2, 5.1, 5.2, 5.3

WHEN implementing a change solution, we learn quickly that monitoring is an everyday action by those in the system. Whether it is administrators or teachers, we strive for compliance to the non-negotiables of the change solution. In the early months of the implementation, we find misunderstandings and confusion about certain aspects of the solution which require our attention to clarify and reset expectations. Our goal is a total quality management principle which is to get a more consistent result by reducing variation in the system. Once we establish the non-negotiables of the change solution, we know that a consistent implementation will produce more consistent results across all grade and content levels.

In the early stages of the implementation, reviewing the elements of the non-negotiables at every teacher and administrator meeting keeps everyone focused on the criteria for implementation. As those new patterns of behavior emerge, now focusing on student needs rather than adult comfort zones, the change solution gains some momentum and educators begin to celebrate small wins. Educators reinforce new behaviors by paying attention to those efforts and that recognition begins to root them in the daily routine of the classroom and school. Remember the Casey Stengel story earlier in the book about keeping the five who loved him with the 15 on the fence? If everyone is monitoring the implementation of the change solution, the vast majority of educators are making progress with these new behaviors. Teacher conversation is now focused on similar issues, collaborating with their colleagues on how to make adjustments in the process to further improve results.

Ever wonder what happened to the five players who hated Casey Stengel? While he prevented the 15 players on the fence from joining them, they are still in charge of blocking the change solution. These are the individuals who hold onto the old culture of adult comfort zone behaviors and become the naysayers of the change solution. They are usually vocal, inciting doubts that one more change solution will be any better than those before it. They serve as the "lounge lizards," making other teachers uncomfortable when they attempt to change the conversation to change the behaviors. They are the storytellers who describe the days when children came to school ready to learn and principals just let teachers do their jobs. In spite of positive momentum by most educators, these individuals keep the fires of doubt burning.

Daily Difficult Conversations

What we know about human behavior is that when blockers begin to act outside our expectation, the usual response is to ignore them, hoping it will get better. What we know is a more effective strategy is having daily difficult conversations each time we find a variance from our expectation. But confrontation is not a natural skill set for everyone. It has to be learned.

In my teaching years, I worked for a principal who was a good person but subscribed to the theory that if two teachers were not meeting their students after lunch, he would send a memo to all of us, reminding us of this expectation. All he did was make the majority of us angry because we were meeting his expectation and we felt he lacked the courage to confront the two "perpetrators." This is what quality teachers resent in administrators, the inability to have daily difficult conversations with those individuals whom refuse to abide by an administrator's expectations.

In his book *First Days of School (1991)*, authors Harry and Rosemary Wong remind us that when children act outside the procedures we have taught them, we should assume they have not learned the procedure, not that they are behaving badly. So he instructs us in the book to reteach the strategy.

The Three Steps to Teaching Procedures

1. **Explain:** *State, explain, model, and demonstrate the procedure.*

2. **Rehearse:** *Rehearse and practice the procedure under your supervision.*

3. **Reinforce:** *Reteach, rehearse, practice, and reinforce the classroom procedure until it becomes a student habit or routine. (p. 176)*

If we follow that strategy as it relates to teacher behaviors, we should not assume the teacher is noncompliant but that the teacher does not understand the expected teaching behavior. As a result, we teach it again and assume there will be a better understanding of expectations. In that difficult conversation, we bring it to the teacher's attention that their teaching practice is not acceptable, what we expect, and how to do it.

When these daily difficult conversations continue, we know that they involve an elevated emotional intensity because the parties are in disagreement about what is expected. When we confront unacceptable teaching behaviors, we know that a teacher may be thinking that the strategies he/she have used over time have been ineffective, thereby labeling the individual as ineffective. We have to remember that the prior behavior was the best the person knew at the time. Instead of making a value judgment, we must help the individual to understand that there are new, more effective teaching strategies that would bring improved results. Affirming the past without accepting it becomes a part of the emotional intensity that tends to dominate these discussions.

In these daily difficult conversations, differing viewpoints are the basis of the conflict. Teachers may feel the principal does not have the content or grade level expertise he/she has and is not a valid source of knowledge. Administrators must counteract that opinion with other teachers within the grade level who are successfully using those strategies and may be willing to have the teacher visit their classroom. Instructional coaches, who became a part of effective schools that participated in the federal Reading First programs, are another source of assistance.

Here is a potential script:

"Mrs. Smith, in observing your classroom today I observed little or no engaged learning."

"What I observed, Mr. Hanson, is that all children were seated quietly completing the worksheets I had assigned them. As I walked around answering questions, I was helping my students."

"Yes, you were. You are to be complimented for your ability to effectively manage your classroom. However, research teaches us that using more engaging activities will increase learning results. Worksheets are not considered engaging activities. In this world of technology, children are accustomed to being more active in the learning process. May we brainstorm how we might change this activity into one that is more engaging?"

"With all due respect, Mr. Hanson, I think you have other teachers who are not as effective as I am who need your help. I will let you move on to help them. I am doing such fine."

"Mrs. Smith, let's look at your data. What does it tell you?"

"Well, no teacher has all students passing the state assessment."

"But we are talking about your students. When I compare their scores from the previous year to this year, many of your students lost ground. That means your teaching had a minimal effect. All students should be growing at least one year in achievement. Some of your student are not. This is why I am suggesting you need to learn some new teaching strategies. What worked before is not working in today's environment."

"Well, I always thought I was effective. Now, all of a sudden, because I am one of the older teachers, I am not doing my job."

"Mrs. Smith, you are doing your job. You have been a valued member of our teaching staff. This is not an indictment of you. It is a request that you add some engaging strategies to your teaching routine that will improve results. I know you want to improve your results, correct?"

"Of course I want to improve. But I am not sure this old dog can learn new tricks."

"I am confident you can. How about observing another teacher using one of these strategies and I will cover your class?"

And so on….

We would like to assume Mrs. Smith observes the teacher and moves forward with new strategies. Our monitoring would determine if she is making the effort, needs more support, or only gave it minimal attention, moving back to her adult comfort levels of old behaviors. Once the administrator notices nothing has changed, he/she must once again have the daily difficult conversation about expectations. Initially, one can assume she did not understand the new procedure and needs further training. So rather than assume the worst, the administrator has a similar conversation as noted above and this time, creates a more aggressive plan with more support for the teacher. He/she will then increase the monitoring for this teacher **to increase her level of discomfort as a motivation to improve.**

The Crucial Confrontation

In spite of efforts to offer support of an educator, provide effective feedback, and model desired behaviors, the situation does not improve. The root cause may be denial by the educator that they are the source of the problem. It may be that the educator does not believe the stated consequences will come to pass. Whatever the situation, the time has now come for the crucial confrontation.

Patterson, Grenny, McMillan, and Switzler added a second book to their series, *Crucial Confrontations: Tools for Resolving Broken Promises, Violated Expectations, and Bad Behavior. (2005)* that moves the dialogue from a conversation about differences of opinion to dealing with disappointment and broken promises. They caution the reader who is preparing for the crucial confrontation to leave anger at the door and begin the conversation by using these steps:

1. **Start with safety.** Demonstrate mutual respect. Establish mutual purpose by establishing your common ground of

wanting what is best for students. Then begin to describe the gap between what you expected and what actually happened. (pp.89-99)

2. **Share your path.** Start with the facts. Explain what, not why. (pp. 100-105)

3. **End with a question.** Ask "what happened?' Then listen carefully. (pp. 106-109.)

The authors remind us as the confrontation process continues, "motivation is about expectations, information, and communication." (p.118)

At some point, the administrator has to decide to begin the process of progressive discipline. The first step is something I developed long ago which is a standard of conduct memo. It describes the unacceptable behavior, lists the expectations by the administrator, and makes it clear that if the unacceptable behavior continues, further discipline can result. It is not a written reprimand but it has a similar effect. The standard of conduct memo effectively documents issues of performance before those issues need serious attention. (**Figure 6.1**)

With most employees, further action by the administrator will not be necessary. For a small percentage of people, this practice will serve as documentation that the employee has been treated fairly and professionally by the supervisor and serves as documentation for further disciplinary action.

It is important to note that once progressive discipline begins, it must be conducted in concert with the district evaluation process. These documents can be attached to an evaluation as data supporting professional conclusions about a teacher.

Further actions include oral reprimands and written reprimands (**Figure 6.2**) as a part of the progressive discipline. Ultimately, unless the behavior is criminal in nature or places students in danger, the progressive discipline will fold into the teacher evaluation process for further consequences.

In the Meantime...

As we confront these behaviors, the day to day activities of

Memorandum

TO: Employee

FROM: Administrator

RE: Standard of Conduct

DATE: ---

The purpose of this memo is to make you aware of a situation that has come to my attention. *(Include as much detail as necessary to define the incident and the alleged lapse in judgment or misconduct by the employee.)* Your behavior in the above mentioned situation is unacceptable to me as your supervisor.

In the future, I expect you to follow the standard of conduct outlined below if a situation similar to this arises. *(List expectations)*

I am confident that you can make the necessary adjustments to meet this standard of conduct expectation. If you have any questions about my expectations of you, please see me immediately.

If the unacceptable behavior noted above reoccurs you could be subject to further disciplinary action.

_____   _____
Employee Signature   Date

_____   _____
Administrator Signature   Date

Original: Personnel file
Copy: Employee
Copy: Administrator

Figure 6.1 Standard of Conduct memo – Mary Rehlander

the school are continuing. It can make the daily interactions uncomfortable. Some teachers will become angry, critical, and openly hostile. These behaviors are not limited to those with whom we are having these conversations. Sometimes the blockers (the five that hate us) may be good teachers who just fight change. In any case, we must know how to handle these behaviors.

We must be mindful that we are not rewarding this unacceptable

DATE:

TO:

FROM:

RE: LETTER OF REPRIMAND

This letter of reprimand is a disciplinary action due to your non-compliance with previous warnings concerning (fill in inappropriate action/s). On (date), we had a conversation that was intended to allow you to correct behavior without receiving a written reminder of the need to meet administrative expectations. Due to an additional incident, which may have been a lack of understanding of the verbal directive, you received a Standard of Conduct Memo indicating, in writing, my expectations.

On (date), you once again.. This continued non-compliance with administrative directives must not continue. Once again, I will outline my expectations for the future:

List expectations

Failure to comply with the expectations explained above could result in further disciplinary action up to and including moving you to the Problem-Solving phase of the evaluation process described in the GOTE plan.

Employee Signature	Date
Administrator Signature	Date

(A signature on this form does not necessarily indicate agreement with the content. It simply indicates that the employee has had discussion with the supervisor and has received a copy of this form.)

Original: Personnel file
Copy: Employee
Copy: Administrator

Figure 6.2 Written Reprimand – Mary Rehlander

behavior by giving it voice. For example, these educators will frequently disrupt faculty meetings by asking questions and then commenting at length about why parents are the problem, or the lack of jobs, etc. If we allow that disruption, we are rewarding the behavior. We can stop the individual as they begin, letting them know they are off topic and you will be happy to speak with them about their issue after the meeting. It is imperative that we treat them with respect when we tell them to hold their comments for after the meeting. If we treat them without respect, we have just moved the 15 players to their side of the fence.

Another strategy may be to put one representative of the push back group on your school improvement committee. Ever hear the saying, "Keep your friends close but your enemies closer?" Keep the naysayer close to you so you know what they are saying. Keeping them close connects you with your diagnostic job of determining what adjustments need to be made in the change effort as a part of the monitoring process. It also allows the administrator or other teachers to negate their impact.

As educators manage this transition, anxiety increases, absences may increase, and people feel overwhelmed as they try to incorporate the change solution into their classroom routine. As they struggle with compliance, the blockers continue to incite discontent. Ignoring this behavior would endanger the change solution implementation by giving the blockers the power to continue to miss commitments and violate expectations. Ignore what you can, stick to the facts, and continue the path to improvement. If you diminish your expectation through your monitoring, you will not see improvement as prescribed in the adopted change effort.

Scenarios

1. Mr. Green is a good teacher as evidenced by his student results. However, he is always "stirring the pot" and creating discontent. How would you harness his potential leadership skills to support the change effort and support teacher efforts?

2. Mr. Peters is a third year teacher who can demonstrate all the classroom management techniques described in *The First Days of School* but the classroom management remains problematic. The administrator has identified these issues in past evaluations and provided professional development through other teachers and the English department chairperson. However, improvement results are not evident. What are your next steps?

3. During a faculty meeting as the principal shares some research on effective teaching, Mrs. Aggravate is grading papers. She is not looking at the handout. Further, when the teachers break into grade level groups, she begins to criticize by asking why her time is being wasted with this activity. As she is disrupting the group, what does the principal do at that moment?

4. The building representative for the teacher's union is not a strong teacher. As the principal is gathering her data, he notices some disturbing trends. Ms. Moment is also a frequent critic of the administrator in the faculty meetings. The principal is concerned about Ms. Moment claiming she is being harassed for her union activities if there is a confrontation about her poor student achievement data. Model the conversation, taking into account the anticipation of countering the charge of retaliation.

CHAPTER SEVEN

STUDENT MONITORING
OF THEIR LEARNING

MOST of our focus, thus far, has been on monitoring by the educators in the system. What we have learned, particularly in the Eight Step Continuous Improvement Process, is that students can effectively monitor their academic progress, once they have been taught the process. Students accepting responsibility for their learning has been a goal of educators for decades!

The first step to teach learners to monitor their performance is to set expectations by sharing the standard expected for mastery. In the Eight Step Process, we use three-week assessments, with four items per standard, to monitor mastery in the three-week calendar window. The system defines mastery as four correct out of four items, with partial mastery at three items out of four, and non-mastery as two, one, or zero items out of four possible correct points. Students become quickly in tune with mastery standards as teachers have them graph their results. (**Figure 7.1**) If you think about traditional grading practices, students have no idea what the acceptable standard will be. So they sit in anticipation of the grade. More importantly, they don't know what to do as a result of a poor grade, other than asking if the teacher will accept extra credit, which distorts the real picture of mastery of the content. In the Eight Step Process, students with non-mastery scores know they will be in a remediation session known as Success Period. They know their teachers will not accept

Student Data Tracking Sheet

Student Name_____

MSD of Warren Township
Indianapolis, IN

2nd Quarter 1st Grade ELA Indiana Academic Standards		Non-Mastery	Partial Mastery	Mastery
1.1.3	Recognize that sentences start with capital letters and end with punctuation, such as periods, question marks, and exclamation points.			✦
1.1.9	Blend 2 to 4 phonemes (sounds) into recognizable words.			✦
1.1.11	Read common sight words.			✦
1.3.3	Confirm predictions about what will happen next in a story.		P	
1.3.4	Distinguish fantasy from reality.			✦
1.3.5	Understand what is read by responding to questions.	✦		⌐
1.4.2	Use various organizational strategies to plan writing.		P	
1.5.1	Write brief narratives (stories) describing an experience.		P	
1.6.1	Print legibly and space letters, words and sentences appropriately		P	

Figure 7.1 Student Graphing of Results

a low score and will expect them to improve. Sadly, most traditional systems do not have the structure to immediately provide corrective instruction to non-mastery students.

A classroom does not have to be an Eight Step classroom for students to monitor their performance. Whether students are graphing their formative assessment results or graphing their homework assignment grades, they can monitor their own results. If students are required to keep track of all grades within a grading period, and the teacher gives them an opportunity to redo assignments or retake a test for improvement, their monitoring of their progress will alert them to whether these opportunities would benefit their results.

Rubrics provide students with performance standards prior to completion of the assignment. Further, they give information to students beyond mastery standards. The rubric defines levels of acceptable performance so students gain an understanding of how the mastery standard evolves. If you think about the typical student, they are not certain what constitutes an "A" or a "C." A rubric gives students the ability to mold their work around the expectations listed in the rubric.

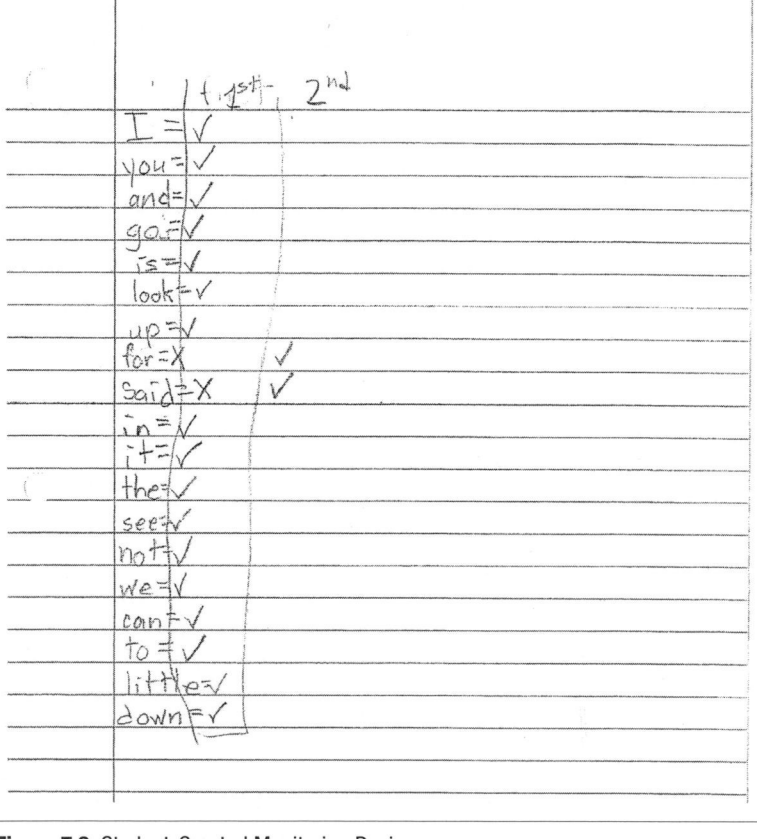

Figure 7.2 Student-Created Monitoring Device

Clever teachers find unique ways to engage students in monitoring themselves and others through their work. A high school mathematics teacher grouped students into pairs. The two worksheets, although using different problems, had the same answers for each numbered problem. Student pairs could monitor themselves because even though the problems were different, if their answers were not the same, they had immediate feedback to go back and rework the problem. Teams could operate without constant monitoring from the teacher.

Another clever example comes from teacher Robin Imai in Everett, Washington Public Schools. In **Figure 7.2**, a fourth grader, working with a new student from Thailand, created her own monitoring document while testing the new student on sight words. As the document demonstrates, she marked those the student did not know and then provided a tutorial with the two words she did not know! This monitoring effort came about without any prompting from the teacher!

For those teachers who engage students in pairs or small group work, the same effective monitoring strategies they use in monitoring the large group will work in those smaller groups where students are leading the learning. Small white boards used with markers, asking for "thumbs up or down" as a response to a question, or having students write questions on a sticky note to share on a board with the group are all legitimate ways for students to monitor themselves and one another.

Cassell and Daggett (2010) define the possibilities of peer learner engagement in their paper, "Peer Learner Engagement: Enhancing the Promise of School Improvement." They acknowledge the research that support peer learning as an effective way to engage students and promote success. They note the following criteria necessary for success:

• *Research-based elements*

• *Close coordination with teacher*

• *Careful monitoring and reinforcement of progress*

• *Intensive and ongoing training*

• *Well-structured and scripted lessons*

• *Frequent and regular tutoring sessions (p.2)*

Student tutoring in pairs or small groups must be carefully planned. He notes that partner work "in which correct and incorrect responses can be clearly determined" (p.5) are most successful. Immediate feedback to the learner, praise, and encouragement are benefits of peer learning in ways adults cannot mirror. Further, sometimes a student can explain something to another student and connect the learning more effectively.

Short student surveys have been used in some of our Eight Step schools for students to reflect upon how the class is operating in their learning activities. When students are prepped about the seriousness in which teachers will use the feedback from them, with a caution that no silly comments will be posted, they can provide telling insight into the classroom effectiveness. Students have been known to respond with "please remove disruptive students who distract my learning" or "activities are boring; can't we do something with computers?" When teachers are comfortable sharing that feedback with students with expectations that they will monitor one another at learning stations or in activities, students generally respond positively. It goes back to rehearse and practice.

Students can effectively monitor their own learning with careful support and structure from teachers. If you think about it, extending the hands of the teacher through peer learning and monitoring that learning, further increases student success.

Scenarios

1. Set up a self-checking activity for a learning station. Remember to put in safeguards for partner work so that students do the work before checking.

2. At the beginning of the grading period, prepare a sheet listing all activities in a content area, possible points, and a blank line for the student to record his/her score. Set up a system for the student to alert the teacher that he/she needs help or would like to redo an assignment.

3. Structure a small group learning area for four-five students. Assign roles as teacher, activity monitor, and checker. Create a review activity where students can teach one another and check for understanding.

4. High school students usually dislike cooperative learning projects. Better students feel they are "carrying" other students. Prepare a cooperative learning activity at differing levels of difficulty. Have students select a project through a sign-up sheet with no more than five students in the group. Set protocols for behavior and teach those before allowing students to begin. What monitoring safeguards will you have to put into place to ensure equitable sharing of the work and accountability for all?

CHAPTER EIGHT

CELEBRATIONS: BY THE INCH, IT'S A CINCH, BY THE YARD IT'S TOO HARD

RECOGNITION is affirmation of effort in producing positive change and is a motivator to continue the effort. Leaders must celebrate every inch of progress whether it is individual praise or praise focused on the group. When we define the smaller steps within the parameters of the change, we must not only pay attention to those that are not implementing, but celebrate those who are making strides toward the change effort.

One of the important elements of charting the course of a change effort is in the identification of the elements of the change and monitoring the implementation. Particularly in the first year of implementation, there is a high level of storming about the change. As I have noted in previous chapters, the key is remembering the first year only happens one time! However, in this age of accountability, we must be able to achieve small wins in the first year for several reasons. First of all, it builds a positive momentum to keep going with the change effort and tends to quiet the doubters. Secondly, when student achievement gains are documented, there are usually positive responses from state or local agencies that are monitoring schools for improvement. Lastly, once the next year is like the past year, teachers and principals gain confidence in implementing the change effort and are encouraged by the positive results.

In the first year of implementation of the Eight Steps in Warren in 2002, we focused on three schools to implement. All K-8 schools implemented the calendars, assessments, and K-5 schools implemented Success Period. Year one was full of pushback, controversy, and refusal to implement properly. One of the three schools, Heather Hills Elementary School, improved its third grade results from 27% to 54% in one year! While they were still low performing, this improvement validated the Eight Steps to others in the district. Heather Hills, and Principal Mary Rehlander, eventually was recognized with the National School Change Award, conferred at Fordham University, for their success in the Eight Steps. The award affirmed the process and all those who implemented it. It was not one big win that impacted student scores. It was the relentless pursuit of implementation of the Eight Steps that eventually led Heather Hills educators to high levels of student achievement.

Jim Collins in his book, *Good to Great (2001),* describes this phenomena as the flywheel effect.

Those who launch revolutions, dramatic change programs, and wrenching restructuring will almost certainly fail to make the leap from good to great. No matter how dramatic the end result, the good-to-great transformation never happened in one fell swoop. There was no single defining action, no grand program , no one killer innovation, no solitary lucky break, no miracle moment. Rather, the process resembled relentlessly pushing a giant heavy flywheel in one direction, turn upon turn, building momentum until a point of breakthrough, and beyond. (p.14)

This flywheel effect reinforces that change efforts are one small step at a time, pushing forward to make progress.

As schools make improvement, it is important to celebrate that achievement with students and staff alike. A school assembly, pep bands, and ice cream treats are perfect for celebrating improvement of student achievement results. We think nothing of pep assemblies to celebrate state athletic championships. Why not celebrate the achievement of learning goals in the same manner? After all, schools are learning organizations.

Further, administrators need to affirm every teacher who made positive improvements in a special way. Nothing should be done to embarrass any one teacher who did not achieve improvement. That is a critical conversation for another day. We are building capacity among our staff in building their confidence in implementing the change effort. Building that capacity is ultimately the key to sustaining the change effort. Affirmation of educators should be as a group with additional attention to the individual contributions made by teachers in private ways. The most powerful dynamic is when teachers celebrate and congratulate one another.

As a result, the celebration of those small steps as well as the actual results, however incremental in nature, is an important step in the improvement effort. Principals can affirm and celebrate incremental progress in teacher behaviors by speaking affirmatively with the teacher, sending a positive note or email, or noting the progress as a formal part of the evaluation document. Paying attention to what matters and celebrating those improvements is the role of the leader. If we don't acknowledge those efforts, teachers fall away from the elements of the change effort. People respect what we inspect, as the old saying goes.

I believe it is also important to celebrate problem solving as a part of capacity building of the school. When teachers focus on a problem, usually in response to data, leaders must help them engage in problem solving. Problems should be solved at the level they most closely affect. As a result, we must empower teachers to solve those problems that impact their teams. Celebrating that effort can be done at a faculty meeting where the teachers define the problem, share the possible solutions, describe the one they selected, and share the results. When we give educators the tools to solve problems related to the implementation of the change effort, we are not lessening expectations. We are making adjustments in the implementation to move it forward.

Many schools celebrate all efforts related to state assessments with pep rallies, videos featuring principals as aliens and teachers in cheerleading gear, and T-shirts for all children. The T-shirts usually encourage children to focus, do their best, and work hard. This testing preparation is not limited to elementary schools. Warren Central High School created two superheroes, Wes and Les, who appeared during the live daily TV program to encourage proper study habits by Wes, but typically poorly modeled by Les, as students prepared all year for end of course assessments required for graduation. And guess who played the superheroes in costume…teachers!

Schools do not wait for the state testing results to celebrate. They celebrate the activities that contribute to the end result of passing state assessments. Honor roll ice cream socials, no discipline referral lunch treats, and thermometers outside of each classroom measuring daily attendance during the countdown calendars prior to state assessments are all examples of celebrating the small steps to the final goal. Principal Patrick Anderson of Pleasant Run Elementary purchased rubber band bracelets, popular among youth today, for each math operation. Once students mastered addition, subtraction, multiplication, or division they came down for their bracelet. Our only limit is our imagination. We know that when we celebrate the small steps to the ultimate goal, we are reinforcing their importance. By the inch (small steps) it's a cinch, by the yard (too large steps) it's too hard. Celebrations reinforce what is important to us in our school culture.

CHAPTER NINE

MAINTAINING MOMENTUM AND BUILDING OWNERSHIP WITHIN THE CULTURE

ELCC Building and District Level Standards: 1.3, 2.2, 2.3, 2.4

CHANGE efforts begin to falter when leadership fails to realize that **maintaining momentum is a forever after activity**. It never stops. Because once the school leadership stops monitoring the change effort, even after year one or two, teachers assume that change effort is no longer the priority. So they allow their teaching behaviors to drift back to adult comfort zones and less effective strategies of old.

Further, schools and school districts are guilty of random acts of school improvement. I call it "flavor of the month" mentality. Some leaders believe that we must implement something new every year to address achievement issues. These are usually programs, not change processes, which are usually short lived. More importantly, the teacher plate of school improvement activities after a few years is overloaded. Teachers do not know the priority because leadership usually identifies the next change effort, provides the training, wishes the teachers well, and never checks again. They become so overwhelmed that their survival is to revert to whatever they can manage. This becomes an individual determination, violating the quality principle that reducing variation in the system gives us a more consistent result. We are back to the idea that classrooms are like flea markets, and teachers are renting a space to shut the door and conduct whatever education they deem appropriate. And we wonder why nothing ever gets better.

Reeves (2011) labels these yearly new efforts, *initiative fatigue*. "The research reveals that *initiative fatigue* is a serious and growing problem. By "initiative fatigue" I mean the tendency of educational leaders and policymakers to mandate policies, procedures, and practices that must be implemented by teachers and school administrators, often with insufficient consideration of the time, resources, and emotional energy required to begin and sustain the initiatives." (p.1) Is it any wonder why teachers roll their eyes and say, "This too shall pass."

Phil Talbert, principal of Hawthorne Elementary School in Warren, tells the story of the daily box of energy. He believes that energy source is finite. We have to decide each day where we will expend that energy. Will we waste it complaining about parents or students who come to school unprepared? Or do we spend our limited energy on the effective strategies that move students into mastery of the materials we are teaching? Once the energy is expended, it is gone.

The first step to improvement is to conduct a cleansing of change initiatives. Reeves (2011) calls it weeding the garden to achieve focus. Leadership along with teachers must decide what is working based on student achievement data and what is not. If a prior program is not producing the results anticipated, the principal and teachers must determine if this particular program requires further investment to improve results, If not, then the principal and teachers need to declare that effort "dead on arrival" and cleanse expectations from the plates of teachers. Before any principal or superintendent can ask teachers to commit to a change process, they must clear the way. That may mean some sacred cows with no supportive data become the best burgers. We cannot ask teachers to do more. If we want them to focus on our change process, we must create the conditions for success by eliminating the distractions of past programs that are no longer relevant or working.

When I came to Warren in 2001, I promised the administrative staff and teachers as well as the Board of Education that the Eight Step Continuous Improvement Process would be our only focus during my tenure. And in my eleven years as superintendent, that was all we did. Every year at opening day I would stand before my teachers and principals and say, "We are doing the same thing this year as in past years. We remain focused on the Eight Steps." I honestly believe that our success in Warren with the Eight Steps was keeping that promise to my principals and teachers.

When we implement a change effort, it takes time to root the process into the daily routine of a school and school district. As teachers gain confidence in implementation, they begin to cleanse their own teaching practices that conflict with the new change process. Like any skill, when we practice something long enough, we become masters of the work. When teachers and principals are given the time to root a change process, it becomes the way they do their work. It becomes their daily routine. Soon they cannot imagine working any other way.

Fullan (2001) reminds us to anticipate the implementation dip. "The implementation dip is literally a dip in performance and confidence as one encounters an innovation that requires new skills and new understandings." (p.40) As teachers move away from familiar behaviors and try to learn new, more effective ones, they are not only afraid of the change but trying to master the actual skill sets of the new behaviors expected. "Thus leaders who are sensitive to the implementation dip combine styles: they still have an urgent sense of moral purpose, they still measure success in terms of results, but they do things that are more likely to get the organization going and keep it going." (p.41) The implementation dip is not a first year phenomena. It happens at different times for different staff and must always be anticipated every year during the change effort.

What we must do to counter the implementation dip is to take a page from Harry Wong. We must review the non-negotiable elements of the change effort and set expectations. We remind staff of our expectations regarding the details of the non-negotiable elements, such as the ninety minute literacy block modeled after the Daily Five, or how we will teach the procedures for movement of

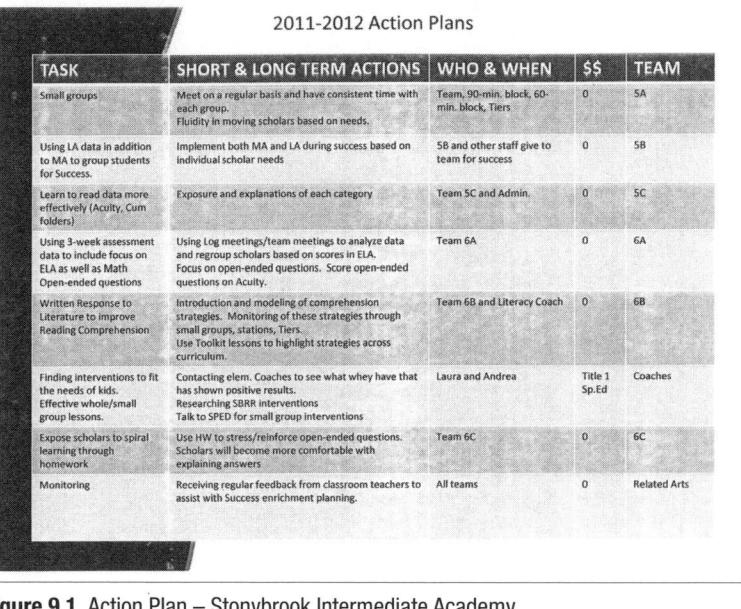

2011-2012 Action Plans

TASK	SHORT & LONG TERM ACTIONS	WHO & WHEN	$$	TEAM
Small groups	Meet on a regular basis and have consistent time with each group. Fluidity in moving scholars based on needs.	Team, 90-min. block, 60-min. block, Tiers	0	5A
Using LA data in addition to MA to group students for Success.	Implement both MA and LA during success based on individual scholar needs	5B and other staff give to team for success	0	5B
Learn to read data more effectively (Acuity, Cum folders)	Exposure and explanations of each category	Team 5C and Admin.	0	5C
Using 3-week assessment data to include focus on ELA as well as Math Open-ended questions	Using Log meetings/team meetings to analyze data and regroup scholars based on scores in ELA. Focus on open-ended questions. Score open-ended questions on Acuity.	Team 6A	0	6A
Written Response to Literature to improve Reading Comprehension	Introduction and modeling of comprehension strategies. Monitoring of these strategies through small groups, stations, Tiers. Use Toolkit lessons to highlight strategies across curriculum.	Team 6B and Literacy Coach	0	6B
Finding interventions to fit the needs of kids. Effective whole/small group lessons.	Contacting elem. Coaches to see what whey have that has shown positive results. Researching SBRR interventions Talk to SPED for small group interventions	Laura and Andrea	Title 1 Sp.Ed	Coaches
Expose scholars to spiral learning through homework	Use HW to stress/reinforce open-ended questions. Scholars will become more comfortable with explaining answers	Team 6C	0	6C
Monitoring	Receiving regular feedback from classroom teachers to assist with Success enrichment planning.	All teams	0	Related Arts

Figure 9.1 Action Plan – Stonybrook Intermediate Academy

students during Success Period, our daily thirty minutes of tutoring or enrichment. And once those expectations are set, we monitor. Every day. Year after year.

It is powerful for school teams to look at the elements of the change process and assess their progress, creating an action plan to address improvements in their implementation. **Figure 9.1** is the action plan by Stonybrook Intermediate Academy. Principal Chris Gearlds used this document to build his plan of improvement for the year with teachers. The tasks represent specific strategies that would improve their Eight Steps implementation, who is responsible, the timeline, and costs. It leaves as little to chance as possible, to quote my colleague Tony Burchett. Our energy in the box will be focused by all staff on a few issues. As these issues are addressed and adjusted in the process, further rooting of the Eight Steps occurred. It became the way that school conducted the business of learning.

Once schools and districts gain momentum through successful steps on their way to the change outcome, they must not assume the change effort is rooted after one year. Otherwise, adults will drift back to what is in the best interests of the adults and not in the best interests of their students. They key is building ownership among educators for the change effort. Once they own the data as not good or bad data, but the next teaching decision, they assume ownership and continue to make refinements to improve the change effort, not abandon it. And then the change effort becomes institutionalized as the way educators do their work.

Scenarios

1. Think of a current school improvement effort in your school. What data will you examine to determine its effectiveness? If the results are not what you expected, how will you determine if it is a training issue, implementation issue, or that the effort is no longer viable?

2. Prepare a plan for how you will bring new teachers into the expected teaching elements of your school improvement process, including how you will include other teachers as you monitor for the implementation dip.

3. Create a rubric for each element of your school improvement effort with your teachers. Define the levels of implementation within the rubric. Ask teachers to conduct their own self-evaluation against the rubric and create their own personal growth goals.

4. Prepare your back to school PowerPoint on your expectations of teacher engagement in the element of the change initiative with specific about behaviors, procedures, and how you will monitor their engagement.

CHAPTER TEN

DISTRICT LEADERSHIP VS. BUILDING LEADERSHIP: TEAMWORK!

ELCC Building and District Level Standards: 1.1, 1.2, 1.3, 1.4, 1.5, 2.1, 2.2, 2.3, 2.4, 3.1, 3.2, 3.3

DISTRICT leaders, in creating a vision for the change effort, must make certain that their principals understand and buy into the change plan, but also that they have the necessary training to gain confidence in implementing and monitoring the non-negotiable elements. District leaders cannot issue the order of a new change effort and then get out of the way with principals. They must work alongside of them, in classrooms, to understand the implementation struggles and have opportunities to dialogue about implementation issues. So many change efforts fail because principals have no support from the district office. They not only need help with learning the change effort, but advice and counsel to deal with the eventual implementation issues that are rooted in fear, backlash, and those protecting the status quo. Ultimately, our role as superintendents and district office staff is to build capacity among our principals. That is an everyday job, not the once a month principals' meeting.

In this age of accountability, we must shift our thinking from assuming that principals have all the skill sets to deal with the political waters of change to expecting to provide district level support to all of them on an ongoing basis. We must blur the lines of responsibility away from principals running the building and the superintendent running the district. We must build capacity with our building leadership. Systemic change must be done as a team effort. As we build collaboration and collegiality among our principals with the central office, we can take advantage of the strengths of some to teach those with weaker skill sets in certain areas. I have little confidence that the university preparation for principals has even touched the political forces of change, adult learning, using data to make teaching decisions, observation and evaluation of teachers, and the pressure of accountability and removing ineffective teachers. Our principals need and deserve our support to build capacity for school improvement and our emotional support on days when having a crucial confrontation with an ineffective teacher drains the energy of a principal. And if principals are doing their job, they will make mistakes. As superintendents, we must embrace those mistakes, guide them through problem solving, pick them up and brush off their knees, and get them back on track. The job of a principal is a pressure cooker in accountability and very different when my principal in student teaching spent two weeks showing his slides of his Hawaii trip in the office.

As superintendents, we must be willing to surround ourselves with competent administrators who will tell us what we don't want to hear. "Yes" people who pretend the emperor really has new clothes will contribute to the decline of the district. Superintendents with egos too big to hear the truth and determine a proper course of action, without anger but in support of those involved, need to choose another career. Systemic change requires confronting long standing traditions and practices that do not foster student achievement growth. You cannot tell staff you are all about student achievement and then protect the sacred cows. When you protect the status quo to save your own neck, quality principals will leave and go to districts who really want to improve.

Jim Collins provided a comparison chart in his book, *How the Mighty Fall and Why Some Companies Never Give In (2009)* about the leadership team dynamics for companies that are on their way

LEADERSHIP-TEAM DYNAMICS:
ON THE WAY DOWN VERSUS ON THE WAY UP

Teams on the Way Down	Teams on the Way Up
People shield those in power from grim facts, fearful of penalty and criticism for shining light on the harsh realities.	People bring forth unpleasant facts—"Come here, look, man, this is *ugly*"—to be discussed; leaders never criticize those who bring forth harsh realities.
People assert strong opinions without providing data, evidence, or a solid argument.	People bring data, evidence, logic, and solid arguments to the discussion.
The team leader has a very low questions-to-statements ratio, avoiding critical input and/or allowing sloppy reasoning and unsupported opinions.	The team leader employs a Socratic style, using a high questions-to-statements ratio, challenging people, and pushing for penetrating insight.
Team members acquiesce to a decision yet do not unify to make the decision successful, or worse, undermine the decision after the fact.	Team members unify behind a decision once made and work to make the decision succeed, even if they vigorously disagreed with the decision.
Team members seek as much credit as possible for themselves yet do not enjoy the confidence and admiration of their peers.	Each team member credits other people for success yet enjoys the confidence and admiration of his or her peers.
Team members argue to look smart or to improve their own interests rather than argue to find the best answers to support the overall cause.	Team members argue and debate, not to improve their personal position, but to find the best answers to support the overall cause.
The team conducts "autopsies with blame," seeking culprits rather than wisdom.	The team conducts "autopsies without blame," mining wisdom from painful experiences.
Team members often fail to deliver exceptional results, and blame other people or outside factors for setbacks, mistakes, and failures.	Each team member delivers exceptional results, yet in the event of a setback, each accepts full responsibility and learns from mistakes.

Figure 10.1 Leadership Team Dynamics (*How the Mighty Fall,* pp.77-78)

to success versus those companies that are in decline. In **Figure 10.1** from his book, he describes specific behaviors. This chart could be used as an informal audit of your team dynamics with principals. If you decide to use the chart, be very transparent about the results.

In fact, I would have a group of principals compile the results. The discussion will improve your team dynamics and demonstrate to principals that you are serious about being a comprehensive learning organization.

What activities and behaviors engage principals in successful leadership from the district level? Marzano and Waters define research-based principles in their book, *District Leadership that Works: Striking the Right Balance (2009)*. It is a comprehensive review of the necessary behaviors to enable districts to become more effective. They speak to highly coupled organizations regarding achievement and instruction. While buildings have autonomy when it comes to daily activities, the non-negotiable framework of achievement and instruction set by the district cannot be compromised. Each building may need to make adjustments within the boundaries of the framework based on their student data and monitoring of their teachers to improve implementation of the framework. But the authors point out that there is no substantive research to support the autonomy of site-based management.

Marzano and Waters (2009) identify research-supported activities that district leaders should engage. They are as follows:

1. Setting and Monitoring Nonnegotiable Goals for Achievement

   a. Reconstitute State Standards as Measurement Topics or Reporting Topics

   b. Track Student Progress on Measurement Topics Using Teacher-Designed and District-Designed Formative Assessment

   c. Provide Support for Individual Students

   d. Redesign Report Card

2. Setting and Monitoring Nonnegotiable Goals for Instruction

   a. Systematically Explore and Examine Instructional Strategies

   b. Design a Model or Language of Instruction

   c. Have Teachers Systematically Interact About the Model or Language of Instruction

    d. Have Teachers Observe Master Teachers (and each other) Using the Model of Instruction

    e. Monitor the Effectiveness of Individual Teaching Styles

3. Collaborative Goal Setting, Board Alignment, and Allocation of Resources

If superintendents or district office administrators are looking for a comprehensive book to guiding "second order" initiatives (break from the past, lies outside existing paradigms, conflicts with prevailing values and norms, requires the acquisition of new knowledge and skills – p. 105), they will find this book to be an excellent resource. It contains lots of details based on comprehensive research. I am proud to say that most of the outline above is reflective of the Eight Steps Continuous Improvement Process! But any school improvement effort you may be considering should be matched against the above elements.

As Marzano and Waters (2009) provide a comprehensive guide to district leadership building capacity with building level administrators, *Leadership on the Line (2002)* is an excellent resource regarding the psychological and human toll that change and its accompanying politics can drain from an individual or institution. These authors remind us that when we exert real leadership to change things, conflict surfaces, long-held beliefs are challenged, and new ways of doing things are demanded, causing pain. When you are the change agent, the target is on your back. Sometimes leaders do not survive the target on their back professionally. Sometimes there is a personal cost.

In conclusion, as we engage in creating high performing organizations that focus on achievement and instruction to improve student results, we must remember these final words:

- **Singular Focus**
- **Continuous Data Stream**
- **Monitoring Critical Elements**
- **Build Ownership Beyond Yourself**

There is no more noble work on behalf of children. Welcome to the world of monitoring and keeping your finger on the pulse of school improvement!

REFERENCES

Casell, William and Willard R. Daggett, "Peer Learner Engagement: Enhancing the Promise of School Improvement." International Center for Leadership in Education, Rexford, New York, January, 2010.

Chang, Richard Y. and Matthew E. Niedzwiecki, *Continuous Improvement Tools, Volume 1.* Jossey-Bass Pfeiffer, San Francisco, California, 1993.

Collins, Jim, *Good to Great, Why Some Companies Make the Leap... and Other Don't,* Harper Business, New York, New York, 2001.

Collins, Jim, *How the Mighty Fall and Why Some Companies Never Give In.* Harper Collins Publishers Inc., New York, New York, 2009.

Costa, Arthur L. and Robert J. Garmston, *Cognitive Coaching, A Foundation for Renaissance Schools.* Christopher Gordon Publishers, Inc., Norwood, Massachusetts, 2002.

Davenport, Patricia and Gerald Anderson, *Closing the Achievement Gap: No Excuses.* APQC, Houston, Texas, 2002.

Davenport, Patricia, *Are We There Yet? Continuing to Close the Achievement Gap,* APQC, Houston, Texas, 2006.

Fullan, Michael, *All Systems Go: The Change Imperative for Whole System Reform*, Corwin, Thousand Oaks, California and Ontario Principals' Council, Ontario, Canada, 2010.

Fullan, Michael, *Leading in Culture of Change*. Jossey-Bass, San Francisco, California, 2001.

Fullan, Michael, *The Six Secrets of Change: What the Best Leaders Do to Help Their Organizations Survive and Thrive*. Jossey-Bass, San Francisco, California, 2008.

Hattie, John, *Visible Learning*. Routledge, London and New York, 2009.

Heifetz, Ronald A. and Marty Linsky, *Leadership on the Line*. Harvard Business School Press, Boston, Massachusetts, 2002.

Katzenmeyer, Marilyn and Gayle Moller, *Awakening the Sleeping Giant, Helping Teachers Develop as Leaders*. Corwin Press, Thousand Oaks, California, 2001.

Kouzes, J.M. and B.Z. Posner, *Encouraging the heart: A leader's guide to rewarding an recognizing others*. Josey-Bass, San Francisco, 1998.

Lezotte, Lawrence W. and Kathleen M. McKee, *Assembly Required: A Continuous School Improvement System*. Effective Schools Product, Ltd., Okemos, Michigan, 2002.

Marzano, Robert J. and Timothy Waters, *District Leadership That Works, Striking the Right Balance*. Solution Tree Press, Bloomington, Indiana, 2009.

Patterson, Kerry, Joseph Grenny, Ron McMillan, and Al Switzler, *Crucial Conversations: Tools for talking when stakes are high*. McGraw-Hill, New York, 2002.

Patterson, Kerry, Joseph Grenny, Ron McMillan, and Al Switzler, *Crucial Confrontations: Tools for resolving broken promises, violated expectations, and bad behavior*. McGraw-Hill, New York, 2005.

Peters, Thomas J. and Robert H. Waterman, Jr., *In Search of Excellence: Lessons From America's Best-Run Companies*. Harper and Row, New York, New York, 1982.

Reeves, Douglas B., *Finding Your Leadership Focus: What Matters Most for Student Results*. Teachers College Press, New York, New York, 2011.

Wong, Harry K. and Rosemary Tripi Wong, *The First Days of School: How to Be an Effective Teacher*. Harry K. Wong Publications, Sunnyvale, California, 1991.

Workshop Handouts

Lezotte, Larry, *"Designing the Effective Learning System TM,"* Effective Schools Products, Ltd., Okemos, Michigan.

APPENDIX

**Standards for Advanced Programs in Educational Leadership
Condensed from January, 2002 document**
www.npvea.org/ELCC/ELCCStandards

Standard 1.0 – Candidates who complete the program are educational leaders who have the knowledge and ability to promote the success of all students by facilitating the development, articulation, implementation, and stewardship of a school or district vision of learning supported by the school community.

    1.1 Develop a vision

    1.2 Articulate a vision

    1.3 Implement a vision

    1.4 Steward a vision

    1.5 Promote Community Involvement in the Vision

Standard 2.0 – Candidates who complete the program are educational leaders who have the knowledge and ability to promote the success of all students by promoting a positive school culture, providing an effective instructional program, applying best practice to student learning, and designing comprehensive professional growth plans for staff.

    2.1 Promote Positive School Culture

    2.2 Provide Effective Instructional Program

2.3 Apply Best Practice to Student Learning

2.4 Design Comprehensive Professional Growth Plans

Standard 3.0 – Candidates who complete the program are educational leaders who have the knowledge and ability to promote the success of all students by managing the organization, operations, and resources in a way that promotes a safe, efficient, and effective learning environment.

3.1 Manage the Organization

3.2 Manage Operations

3.3 Manage Resources

Standard 4.0 – Candidates who complete the program are educational leaders who have the knowledge and ability to promote the success of all students by collaborating with families and other community members, responding to diverse community interests and needs, and mobilizing community resources.

4.1 Collaborate with Families and Other Community Members

4.2 Respond to Community Interests and Needs

4.3 Mobilize Community Resources

Standard 5.0 – Candidates who complete the program are educational leaders who have the knowledge and ability to promote the success of all students by acting with integrity, fairly, and in an ethical manner.

5.1 Acts with Integrity

5.2 Acts Fairly

5.3 Acts Ethically

Standard 6.0 – Candidates who complete the program are educational leaders who have the knowledge and ability to promote the success of all students by understanding, responding to, and influencing the larger political, social, economic, legal, and cultural context.

6.1 Understand the Larger Context

6.2 Respond to the Larger Context

6.3 Influence the Larger Context

Standard 7.0 – Internship. The internship provides significant opportunities for candidates to synthesize and apply the knowledge and practice and develop the skills identified in Standards 1-6 through substantial, sustained, standards-based work in real settings, planned and guided cooperatively by the institution and school district personnel for graduate credit.